THE TAO OF LOVE

The Ancient Chinese Way to Ecstasy

*Love and food are equally
Vital to our sanity and survival*

Ko Tzu

THE TAO OF LOVE

The Ancient Chinese Way to Ecstasy by JOLAN CHANG

Foreword and *Postscript* by Joseph Needham

AND SEX 阴阳之道

A Dutton Paperback

E. P. DUTTON

NEW YORK

First published 1977
Text copyright © Jolan Chang 1977
Translation copyright © Jolan Chang 1977

For information contact: E.P. Dutton, a division of New
American Library, 2 Park Avenue, New York, N.Y. 10016.

Library of Congress Catalog Number: 76-54578

ISBN: 0-525-48230-X

20 19 18 17 16 15 14

Contents

List of Illustrations

Acknowledgments

The author and publishers would like to thank all those who have given permission for copyright illustrations to be reproduced in this book.

Illustrations from the C.T. Loo Collection, Collection Charles Ratton, Jean Pierre Dubosc Collection and Louis Bataille Collection are all from *The Clouds and the Rain*, original editor Office du Livre, Fribourg. Illustrations from the British Museum are reproduced by courtesy of the Trustees of the British Museum.

Bamboo decorations throughout are adapted from *The Mustard Seed Garden Manual of Painting 1679–1701*.

Thanks are also due to Joseph Needham for permission to reproduce the illustration on the title page and other pictures from his collection and to *Theology* magazine for permission to include Joseph Needham's Address for Caius Chapel (Whit Sunday, 1976).

Foreword

VERY FEW WESTERN SCHOLARS HAVE EVER GIVEN ANY STUDY TO traditional Chinese sexology. Yet the subject itself is necessarily one of absorbing interest for every adult human being; and Chinese culture in particular, with its unique genius for combining the rational and the romantic, would be expected to have important things to say about it.

Apart from the admirable Henri Maspero, one of the greatest of such scholars was Robert van Gulik (quoted from time to time in this book) whom I first met during the war in 1942. He was going out to Chungking as Chargé d'Affaires of the Netherlands, while I was on the way to my post as Scientific Counsellor at the British Embassy there. Later on, if my memory is right, I made the speech at his wedding to Miss Shui Ssu-Fang, which was held in our Science Co-operation mess. Still later, after the war, when I had become involved with Taoism and its search for longevity and immortality, he and I had a long correspondence in which I think I persuaded him that there was nothing perverse or pathological in the sexual techniques described and prescribed by the Taoist adepts. This fitted in with his own conviction, derived from a deep knowledge of the literature, that Chinese sex life through the centuries had been remarkably healthy, free from the aberrations of sadism and masochism,[1] but immensely skilled in happy variation and mutual donation. The present book is entirely in this tradition.

My own copy of the greatest Chinese sexological collection, the *Shuang Mei Ching An Ts'ung Shu*, edited by Yeh Tê-Hui, had been bought, as I recall with pleasure, from a woman bookseller, in the Liu Li Ch'ang in Peking in 1952. Since then I have again devoted study to these topics, since the important *nei tan* or 'inner elixir' part of Chinese alchemy had a great deal to do with sexual techniques which, it was believed, would prolong life and lead perhaps to material immortality.[2]

---

[1] With the exception of the fetichism of the bound-feet custom, unknown before the tenth century, and today entirely a thing of the past.

[2] This account will be appearing before long in collaboration with Dr Lu Gwei-Djen, in Vol. 5, Part 5 of *Science and Civilisation in China* (Cambridge University Press).

Then in 1972 a further luminary appeared in these skies, our friend Chang Chung-Lan (Jolan Chang) from Stockholm, whose book on Chinese — and Universal — sexology I here commend to the candid reader. With considerable learning and skill he has found words to explain to men and women of the modern world something of how the wisdom of Chinese culture manifested itself in the affairs of the heart, in love and sex. Though he deals mainly with technical matters, these must always be seen against that background of wider *sapientia*, startling though it may be for Westerners, the Chinese conviction that there can be no line of distinction between sacred and profane love. This is something needed, surely, by all people everywhere.

JOSEPH NEEDHAM

Preface

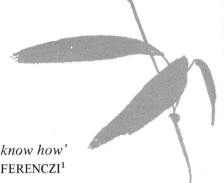

'They want to love one another but they don't know how'
SANDOR FERENCZI[1]

IN HER POPULAR BOOK, *FEAR OF FLYING*, THE FEMINIST ERICA JONG
thoughtfully reflects:

... but the big problem was how to make your feminism jibe with your unappeasable
hunger for male bodies. It wasn't easy. Besides, the older you got, the clearer it
became that men were basically terrified of women. Some secretly, some openly. What
could be more poignant than a liberated women eye to eye with a limp prick? All
history's greatest issues paled by comparison with these two quintessential objects: the
eternal woman and the eternal limp prick.

She continues a moment later: 'That was the basic inequity which could
never be righted: not that the male had a wonderful added attraction called
a penis, but that the female had a wonderful all-weather cunt. Neither storm
nor sleet, nor dark of night could faze it. It was always there, always ready.
Quite terrifying, when you think about it. No wonder men hated women.
No wonder they invented the myth of female inadequacy.'

I could not agree more when she said: 'All history's greatest issues paled
by comparison . . .', but feel that she gave up hope too soon to say
' . . . which could never be righted'. The ancient Taoists found a way thousands of years ago. In fact many Taoists and some fortunate non-Taoists
are applying it right now all over the world. What is unfortunate is that
the knowledge has never been greatly disseminated — a fact which this
book hopes to help to remedy. In this preface two important questions
should also be answered. One morning last winter at his beautiful southern
retreat in France, the famous author Lawrence Durrell urged that I must tell
how I became a Taoist and what prompted me to write the book. The
following is an outburst of idealism inspired by a novelist's eternally
searching mind.

A mother does much more than give her child life. She is a most powerful
formative influence, and shapes her child's future for good or evil, for joyful
living or sorrowful self-destruction.

---

[1]   Quoted in Karl Menninger, *Man Against Himself* (Harcourt Brace and World, New York), p.381.

In this respect I am extremely fortunate. My mother was a woman of great understanding, zest and compassion and, though I did not realize it for many years, the most natural Taoist I have ever met.

When I say 'natural' I mean that, without professing Taoism or even being aware of being one, she created an atmosphere and environment in which a Taoist attitude prevailed. Being brought up in such an atmosphere, I too became a natural Taoist except that I became aware of the fact at the age of about twelve.

A Taoist usually has boundless love for the Universe and all the lives in it. Any form of waste and destruction is to a Taoist evil and must be prevented. With this background it is understandable that I should have searched for ways to remedy the violence and destruction which are so widespread, and for the reasons why so many seemingly very successful people voluntarily do away with themselves: Ernest Hemingway, George Sanders, Mark Rothko ... the list is endless. And why thousands of healthy men and women, even children, slowly destroy themselves by smoking, drugs, alcohol and unhealthy eating and living habits. Why many more thousands of people so hate everyone and everything in sight that they wish − or even try − to destroy them all. And finally, why man's history is a story of endless wars. For the glories of conquest, or just for bottomless greed? Or for power?

From my early teens I have been wondering and seeking answers to these questions. After years of travelling to many continents, meeting thousands of people of different nationalities and exploring all the important philosophies and religions of the world, I came to realize that these evils have their root in the failure of men and women to achieve the fundamental harmony of Yin and Yang; and that in Taoism was to be found an answer which was both easy and pleasant.

Why is it an easy way? Because it has no formality, no dogma, no church. And all it asks one to do is to relax, be natural.

And why is it so pleasant? Because it does not ask one to give up any earthly or heavenly joys, such as music or beauty, as did the ancient Chinese philosophy of Mohism (an altruistic philosophy contemporary with Confucianism, not to be confused with Maoism). Nor does it ask one to reject all desire − such as the craving for beauty of form, sound, smell, taste, touch and carnal love − as do nearly all the schools of Buddhism. On the contrary, Taoism advises one to cultivate better taste, healthy living, and to enjoy earthly or heavenly joys more fully. To the Taoist there are no dividing lines between earthly and heavenly joys: they unite in ecstasy, for in the enjoyment of things natural or artistic, the Taoist is in communion with the Universe (his term for God).

As I have personally experienced in my own life Taoism believes that there can be no solution to any of the world's problems without a wholesome approach to love and sex. Nearly all destruction or self-destruction, almost all hatred and sorrow, almost all greed and possessiveness, spring from starvation of love and sex. And yet the source and fountain of love and sex is as inexhaustible as the Universe itself. This is not my own original idea; it is merely an attempt to revive what the ancient Taoists knew for thousands of years — that without the harmony of Yin and Yang, the fountainhead of life and joy, nothing is left for us but death and destruction.

Stockholm 1976   JOLAN CHANG

Chapter One

The Tao of Loving

In managing affairs there is no better advice than to be sparing
To be sparing is to forestall.
To forestall is to be prepared and strengthened.
To be prepared and strengthened is to be ever successful.
To be ever successful is to have infinite capacity.[1]

TWO THOUSAND YEARS AGO, IF NOT MUCH EARLIER, THE CHINESE TAOIST physicians were writing frank, explicit books on love and sex. They were neither prurient nor self-conscious, because they regarded love-making as necessary to the physical and mental health and well-being of both men and women. In keeping with this philosophy, they placed strong emphasis on sexual skills. Everything was done to further man's loving prowess. Literature and art were produced illustrating sexual techniques. A husband who could enjoy frequent and prolonged sexual intercourse was more highly rated than one who was merely young and handsome. To the Taoist physicians love-making was considered a part of the natural order of things. Sex was not only to be enjoyed and savoured but was considered wholesome and life-preserving. In order to keep people proficient in loving a number of methods were formulated and erotic pictures were used both to instruct and titillate men and women. In their book *Erotic Art* Phyllis and Eberhard Kronhausen quote a poem written by Chang Hêng about A.D. 100 which describes how a bride uses an erotic guidebook to make her wedding night a memorable one:

> Let us now lock the double door with its golden lock,
> And light the lamp to fill our room with its brilliance,
> I shed my robes and remove my paint and powder,
> And roll out the picture scroll by the side of the pillow,
> The Plain Girl[2] I shall take as my instructress,

---

[1] *Tao Tê Ching*, Chapter 59.
[2] i.e. Su Nü, see pp.17-18, 30-32, 44, 50-51, 70-71, 74-5, 79, 83-4, 92-3.

So that we can practise all the variegated postures,
Those that an ordinary husband has but rarely seen,
Such as taught by T'ion-lao to the Yellow Emperor.
No joy shall equal the delights of this first night,
These shall never be forgotten, however old we may grow.[3]

Later on the Kronhausens describe how erotic art was used in ancient China:

We have to turn to Chinese erotic literature to appreciate how the picture albums were used. In one of the best erotic novels of the Ming dynasty, *Jou P'u T'uan*,[4] we find, for instance, the description of the amorous adventures of a young and gifted scholar, Wie-yang-sheng. He marries a well-educated and beautiful girl, Yu-Hsiang ['Jade Perfume'], whose only fault lies in the sad fact that she is excessively prudish: she only agrees to sexual intercourse in the dark and refuses every sexual technique that deviates from the routine. To his further dismay, the bridegroom also notices that Jade Perfume never reaches orgasm during their marital love-making.

To remedy this situation, the young husband decides to purchase a costly album of erotic pictures with which he hopes to educate his wife and change her attitude. Jade Perfume, as might be expected, at first refuses to even look at the pictures, much less let herself be influenced by them. However, in the end she agrees to study them under her husband's guidance, 'her passion becomes greatly aroused' by them, and she gradually turns into the warm, sensuous, and fully responsive woman that her name implies.[5]

The current Western attitude towards erotic pictures or so-called 'pornography' had no place in ancient China. The distinctive ancient Chinese approach to love and sex was also noted by the eminent scholar-diplomat R.H. van Gulik, who wrote a book called *Sexual Life in Ancient China*. In it he said: 'It was probably this mental attitude (considering the sexual act as part of the order of nature ... it was never associated with a feeling of sin or moral guilt) together with the nearly total lack of repression that caused ancient Chinese sexual life to be, on the whole, a healthy one, remarkably free from the pathological abnormality and aberrations found in so many other great ancient cultures.'[6]

But it was not only the ancient Chinese attitude towards sex that surprised and interested van Gulik; it was also the ancient Taoist concept of love-making. This concept, which we call the 'Tao of Loving', has never been described accurately and in detail for Western readers. On the face of it the Tao of Loving seems to represent a very different practice from nearly all accepted Western views on sex and love-making. It is easy to reject it out

[3]   Phyllis and Eberhard Kronhausen, *Erotic Art*, p.24.
[4]   *The Prayer-Mat of the Flesh.*
[5]   P. and E. Kronhausen, *op. cit.*, pp.241 and 242.
[6]   R.H. van Gulik, *Sexual Life in Ancient China*, p.51.

of hand just as the West long rejected acupuncture, now recognized as a great analgesic technique. Today, centuries later, Western doctors are astonished at what it can accomplish and are trying to learn its secrets. The Tao of Loving has its own secrets to reveal to the West. Here is how van Gulik describes it: '[The Tao of Loving theories] have throughout the ages formed the fundamental principle of Chinese sexual relations, so the curious conclusion is that for more than two thousand years coitus reservatus [his term for the Tao of Loving] must have been widely practised in China without apparently affecting adversely the progeniture or the general health of the race.' [7]

Van Gulik was obviously trying to be fair. He was forced to admit that the Chinese were a hardy and long-lived race and all this despite their seemingly revolutionary sex practices.

Even today the Tao of Loving seems revolutionary. But with every new discovery by Western sexologists and scientists, its precepts become more acceptable. The basic principles of the Tao — regulation of ejaculation, the importance of female satisfaction, and the understanding that male orgasm and ejaculation are not necessarily one and the same thing — have become important points in the Women's Liberation Movement and in the scientific studies of Kinsey, Masters and Johnson, and the rest. As their theories come to be accepted in the West, the concept about love and sex, which began so long ago in China, will once again have come full circle. Even when van Gulik wrote his book, he was struck by the way in which modern research was beginning to confirm what the Tao of Loving masters had taught: 'I may draw attention here to the fact that the description of the "five signs" [in observing the woman's satisfaction] as found in the *I Hsin Fang* [a tenth-century medical book which consists of extracts from several hundred Chinese works of the T'ang period and earlier] agrees in all detail with that given in A.C. Kinsey's *Sexual Behaviour of the Human Female* (section "Physiology of sexual response and Orgasm" pp.603, 604, 607 and 613). This does credit to the ancient Chinese sexologists.'[8]

The 'five signs' of female satisfaction van Gulik mentioned appeared a couple of thousand years earlier in a dialogue supposed to have taken place between the Emperor Huang Ti[9] and his chief female advisor Su Nü:

Emperor Huang Ti: 'How does a man observe his woman's satisfaction?'

[7] R.H. van Gulik, *op. cit.*, p.47.
[8] R.H. van Gulik, *op. cit.*, p.156.
[9] The historicity of Huang Ti is uncertain. His traditional dates in the Third Millennium B.C. are not accepted today. But the texts here given may well be of Han (206 B.C.–A.D. 219) origin.

Su Nü: 'There are five signs, five desires and ten indications. A man should observe these signs and react accordingly. The five signs are:

(1) Her face is flushing red and her ears are hot. This indicates that thoughts of making love are active in her mind. The man can now start coition gently in a teasing manner, thrust very shallowly and wait and watch for further reactions.

(2) Her nose is sweaty and her nipples become hard. This signifies that the fire of her lust is somewhat heightened. The jade peak can now go in to the depth of the "Valley's Proper" [five inches] but not much deeper than that. The man should wait for her lust to intensify before going in deeper.

(3) When her voice is lowered and sounds as though her throat is dry and hoarse, her lust has intensified. Her eyes are closed and her tongue sticks out and she pants audibly. That is the time that the man's stalk of jade can go in and out freely. The communion is now gradually reaching an ecstatic stage.

(4) Her "Red Ball" [vulva] is richly lubricated and her fire of lust is nearing its peak and each thrust causes the lubricant to overflow. Lightly his jade peak touches the Valley of "Water-Chestnut Teeth" [depth: two inches]. And then he can use the thrusting method of one left, one right, one slow and one quick, or any other method, freely.

(5) When her "Golden Lotus" [feet] stick up high in the manner of hugging the man, her fire and lust have now reached their peak. She wraps her legs around his waist and two hands hold his shoulder and back. Her tongue remains sticking out. These are the signs that the man should now thrust deeper up to the "Valley of the Deep Chamber" [six inches]. Such deep thrusts will make her ecstatically satisfied throughout her body.'

Although the ancient Chinese studies are couched in flowery and poetic rather than clinical language, this does not mean that their authors were not serious about the subject of love and sex. In fact they thought that good health (mental and physical) and longevity were closely linked to love-making. Because of this, love and sex was considered an important branch of medicine. Its benefits in no way detract from its pleasures. Far from it. Intrinsic to the Tao of Loving was the idea that love and sex could only be properly beneficial when it was totally satisfying.

1. *What is Tao?*

> *A huge tree grows from a tiny sprout,*
> *A nine-storey tower rises from a heap of earth,*
> *A thousand-mile journey begins from one's feet.* [10]

In order to understand the ancient Taoist way of loving we must first have some idea of Tao — the fountainhead from which the Tao of Loving springs. It is a philosophy which has served the Chinese well and has strengthened

[10] *Tao Tê Ching*, Chapter 64.

their innate hardiness with its precepts of prudence and good timing. There is an old saying that 'If Confucianism is the outer garment of the Chinese, Taoism is its soul.' The durability of the Sinic civilization certainly owes much to its teachings, which counselled patience and harmony in poetic analogies:

> *Stretch (a bow) to the utmost,*
> *And you'll wish you had stopped in time.*
> *Temper (a sword) to its very sharpest,*
> *And the edge will not last long.* [11]

Tao itself is a native wisdom which began many thousands of years ago. No one knows exactly when. However, in the sixth century B.C., Lao Tzu compiled its basic precepts into a book which he called the *Tao Tê Ching.* It runs to a little more than five thousand words, making it probably the shortest important book in the world. It has been translated into many languages and there are more than thirty versions in English alone. Each translator has understood and interpreted Lao Tzu's words somewhat differently; but basic to the Taoist philosophy is the belief that energy and momentum are the sources of all life. In the universal scheme of things we human beings are tiny, insignificant and vulnerable creatures. Unless we are in harmony with these sources − the infinite force of nature − we cannot hope to last long. This is the essential point of the *Tao Tê Ching.* The Tao *is* the infinite force of nature. The philosophy of Tao is to endure. To practise Tao one must be truly relaxed and natural in order to become a part of this infinite force. It was from this natural philosophy of prudence, conservation and flexibility that the Tao of Loving developed.

Taoism itself has always been of interest to Western philosophers. More recently scientists and doctors have shown an interest. In 1929 the psychiatrist C.G. Jung wrote an Introduction to a book on Taoism, and in his own collected works Jung includes an essay that deals with the Tao. He says:

Because the things of the inner world influence us all the more powerfully for being unconscious it is essential for anyone who intends to make progress in self-culture to objectivate the effects of the anima and then try to understand what contents underlie those effects. In this way he adapts to, and is protected against, the invisible. No adaptation can result without concessions to both worlds.

From a consideration of the claims of the inner and outer worlds, or rather, from the conflicts between them, the possible and the necessary follows. Unfortunately our

---

[11] *Ibid.*, Chapter 9.

Western mind, lacking all culture in this respect, has never yet devised a concept, nor even a name, for the 'union of opposites through the middle path', that most fundamental item of inward experience, which could respectably be set against the Chinese concept of 'Tao'.[12]

Jung went on to describe his own psychiatric technique as being similar to the Chinese goals and methods. Both the Taoists and Jung were searching for a path towards harmonious living. And a vital part of this is the Tao of Loving.

2. *The similarity between ancient and modern sex studies*

As I have already remarked, the ancient Chinese scholars and physicians studied and discussed sex and sexual practices in much the same way as Masters and Johnson and Kinsey have done in our time. And many of the conclusions of the ancient Chinese are currently being reaffirmed by modern science. For instance, Masters and Johnson are the first modern sex researchers to approve of repeated interruptions in the sex act in order to prolong coition, enabling the female to be thoroughly satisfied and the male partner gradually to learn to control his ejaculation.

This agrees almost entirely with the ancient Chinese texts on the Tao of Loving which actually teach this kind of ejaculation control.

In their report, Masters and Johnson recommend what they call a 'squeeze technique' to help men who suffer from premature ejaculation. It is a rather elaborate technique: the woman must be in the female superior position and when he tells her he has reached the 'danger level' she must quickly elevate herself from the penile shaft and squeeze his penile head for three or four seconds. This will make him lose the urge to ejaculate.

The ancient Chinese 'squeeze technique' is in theory remarkably similar to the Masters and Johnson version – but much simpler to carry out. It can be used in nearly all love positions because the man applies the pressure to himself. (For a fuller discussion of this technique, see pp.41–2.)

Again, Masters and Johnson are the first Western scientists to sanction indefinite delay of male ejaculation: 'Many males learn to restrain or delay their ejaculation until their partner is satiated. Satiation on the woman's part may represent several complete cycles of sexual response with the consequent demand for maintained penial erection for an extended period of time ... thus, the primary stage of penial involution, usually a rapid process, may be extended indefinitely and second stage penial involution subsequently delayed. No acceptable physiological explanation can be

[12] C.G. Jung, *Collected Works*, Vol. 3, translated by R.F.C. Hull, p.203.

offered at present for this clinical observation.'[13]

Their open-minded attitude differs from the Tao of Loving only in degree. The Tao actually urges all men to develop ejaculation control and considers it beneficial to both sexes.

Perhaps the most startling conclusion Masters and Johnson arrived at in their research was that a man need not ejaculate every time he makes love. This rule is especially important when a man reaches fifty. Masters has said that he considers this the single most important point in their second book, *Human Sexual Inadequacy*. He goes on to say that if an older man can accept this advice, 'he is potentially a most effective sexual partner'.[14]

The Tao of Loving agrees with this entirely and, in fact, develops the point even further. A seventh-century physician, Li Tung Hsüan, the director of a medical school in Ch'ang-an, the Imperial capital, had this to say in his book *T'ung Hsüan Tzu*: 'A man should cultivate the ability to delay his ejaculation until his love partner is fully satisfied . . . A man should discover and master his own ideal ejaculatory frequency. And this should not be more than two or three times in ten coitions.'[15]

3. *Ejaculation reconsidered*

Another seventh-century physician, Sun S'sû Mo, set the age limit at forty instead of fifty. After that age, he felt, a man must be very careful not to force ejaculation. Nearly every ancient Tao of Loving text warns against forcing ejaculation. Along with this, the ancient Taoists taught that male orgasm and ejaculation *were not one and the same thing*. Fewer ejaculations in no way meant a man was sexually inadequate nor that he would experience less sexual pleasure. Calling ejaculation 'the climax of pleasure' is really just a habit. And a harmful habit at that. A dialogue between one of Huang Ti's Tao of Loving advisors and a Tao of Loving master which appeared in an ancient book called *Yü Fang Pi Chüch* (or 'The Secrets of the Jade Chamber') may help to explain this point:

Tsai Nü [one of Huang Ti's three female Tao advisors] : 'It is generally supposed that a man derives great pleasure from ejaculation. But when he learns the Tao he will emit less and less, will not his pleasure also diminish?'

P'êng Tsu [Huang Ti's senior Tao advisor] : 'Far from it. After ejaculation a man is tired, his ears are buzzing, his eyes heavy and he longs for sleep. He is thirsty and his limbs

[13] Masters and Johnson, *Human Sexual Response*, p.185.
[14] Masters and Johnson, *Human Sexual Inadequacy*, Chapter 12.
[15] *T'ung Hsüan Tzu*, Chapter 12.

inert and stiff. In ejaculation he experiences a brief second of sensation but long hours of weariness as a result. And that is certainly not a true pleasure. On the other hand, if a man reduces and regulates his ejaculation to an absolute minimum, his body will be strengthened, his mind at ease and his vision and hearing improved. Although the man seems to have denied himself an ejaculatory sensation at times, his love for his woman will greatly increase. It is as if he could never have enough of her. And this is the true lasting pleasure, is it not?'

People often ask me what is my pleasure when I emit only about once out of every hundred copulations. My usual answer is: 'I certainly will not change my joy for your kind of pleasure. And I have experienced twelve long years[16] with your type of ejaculatory pleasure and that is twelve years too long and wasted!' If the inquirer is a man he cannot really doubt my sincerity because I look so peaceful, happy and healthy and so very fond of making love. And if the inquirer is a woman partner who feels sorry for me at the very beginning of our relationship, my enthusiasm in loving her will soon overcome her doubt that I am enjoying myself with her greatly. In any case in a duration of a few hours she will discover that she is experiencing an entirely new way of loving and she will most likely realize that she has never enjoyed love as much before. In fact many women have been generous enough to tell me that they never knew that making love could be such an ecstatic delight.

How does a Tao of Loving adept manage this? And how do I enjoy my loving with so few emissions?

I must tell you some of my own experiences before I can make you understand all this. I was born in one of the most romantic provinces of China, and the capital of the province Hangchow is indisputably the city in the most beautiful setting in China. Marco Polo describes it as the most noble city in the world (in his book the city is named Kingsay). And that is great praise indeed for a man from the beautiful city of Venice! The city was the old capital of the most artistic Southern Sung Dynasty. Even today a great proportion of Chinese writers and poets are from its vicinity. In April and May the whole city, especially around the lake, has the atmosphere of a euphoric dream. The lake itself is named after Shi Tzu (Shi Shih), perhaps the most beautiful woman in Chinese history who was born just across the river of the city several hundred years before Christ. And one of the hills around the lake is named after the famous Taoist Ko Hung, whom we shall mention from time to time in this book. Many years of my childhood were spent in that city and near that beautiful lake.

And what was the result? I became interested in beautiful women when I

---

[16] See Summing Up, p.117.

was only about seven. As all sexologists will tell you, men start practising their love life with masturbation. I did when I was about twelve or thirteen, but it did not please me at all. Perhaps I was spoiled by beautiful natural scenery, literature and poems.

I felt masturbation was too mechanical an act and there was no poetry in it. And I believe I must be one of the few men who have not masturbated more than a dozen times in their whole life. I often wonder how so many sexologists could call this boring, monotonous act a 'joy of sex'? And no wonder that no Taoist ever thinks the subject even worthy of mentioning.

Real coition with a woman did not happen to me until I was about eighteen. It is not that there were no opportunities but to learn how to take advantage of them took a long time. And my first coitions disappoint-ed me nearly as much as my brief adventure in masturbation. As I said a short while ago, I ejaculated — or masturbated in vagina (as I now regard it) — for about twelve years. I do not regard it as a great pleasure for several reasons: (1) the man is constantly anxious about his ejaculation; (2) the woman often worries about getting pregnant; (3) if she takes pills or is equipped with a coil she is constantly worried about the side-effects, and if she uses all the other implements she has to think about fitting them in time. How can a man and woman really realize poetic ecstasy with all those worries on their minds?

Now compare it with a man who has mastered the Tao. First of all he and his partner are free: free of all the worries we have just mentioned. Additionally they are free to make love whenever they have time and feel like it. They can make love so much longer and oftener that they have enough time to appreciate and savour each other's skin texture, curved lines and personal seductive smells, etc. This is not possible if one has worries on one's mind.

Unless he uses the Tao of Loving methods a man is like a gourmet who would love to eat his favourite dish constantly but unfortunately he cannot because the capacity of his stomach will not allow it. The poor Romans loved their food so much they habitually made themselves sick so that they could repeat their eating — that in my view is neither a healthy, an economical nor an aesthetic practice. But a couple who have mastered the Tao can have their favourite loving dishes all the time.

I am aware that none of this really answers the question: what is it like to have sex without ejaculation?

In a sense the question is as unanswerable as the question 'What is blue?'

asked by a blind man. All I can do is to ask in response another question: 'What is ejaculation like?' Surely the answer to that question is that ejaculation is a release of tension in an explosive way. Like a shout of rage or a burst of laughter or . . .

If that is true, then I can say that sex without ejaculation is also a release of tension but without the explosion. It is a pleasure of peace not of violence, a sensuous and lastingly satisfying melting into something larger and more transcendent than oneself. It is a feeling of wholeness, not of separation; a merging and a sharing not an exclusive, private and lonely spasm.

Beyond that, it eludes words.

4. *The harmony of Yin and Yang*

The utmost emphasis laid upon regulating ejaculation according to a man's age and condition of health, etc., was not an arbitrary point adopted by Tao of Loving masters but a conclusion, reached after hundreds of years of careful observation, that male semen was one of the vital essences and must not be squandered in an uncontrolled manner. Sun S'sû-Mo, the most prominent physician of the T'ang (A.D. 618–906) period, has this to say in his *Priceless Recipe*: 'When a man squanders[17] his semen, he will be sick and if he carelessly exhausts his semen he will die. And for a man this is the most important point to remember.'

Once a man has acquired the ability to regulate his ejaculation, not only is his vital essence conserved, he gains much more besides. First his love partner will no longer be dissatisfied because he will now have more confidence in himself and will be able to make love almost as often as he and his partner want to. And, because they can make love much more often and much longer, the partners benefit more fully from each other's essence: he from her Yin essence and she from his Yang essence. As a result they can achieve a unique degree of peace of mind. This tranquillity, due to constant warm and joyful loving, was known to the ancient Chinese as 'the harmony of Yin (female) and Yang (male)'. In this book, we will try to show you how to achieve this Yin/Yang harmony, what we call the Tao of Loving (which was also in ancient times called the 'Tao of Yin and Yang', the 'Tao of Communion' or 'Yin/Yang Communion').

---

[17] 'Squandering' here means using one's resources carelessly beyond one's means.

5. *The similarity between ancient and modern in the theory of harmony and happiness*

Nearly thirty years ago René Spitz, Professor of Psychiatry at the University of Colorado Medical School, discovered that more than 30 per cent of the babies at orphanages do not survive their first year of the impersonal, loveless institutional life, regardless of adequate food, materially hygienic surroundings and excellent medical care. And in recent years, the noted Swiss child psychologist Jean Piaget has emphasized the vital importance of loving/touching and communication to the well-being and healthy growth of infants.

Such loving/touching and communication are equally vital to adult men and women. And this has only lately been popularized in the West by, among others, Masters and Johnson in their third book, *The Pleasure Bond*. They feel that human happiness and well-being are almost unattainable without regular loving/touching between adult men and women. This of course is very similar to the Yin-Yang harmony we are talking about in this book except that the ancient Taoists emphasized the importance of the man acquiring the ability to regulate his emission.

This stress laid by the Tao upon ejaculation control is to provide the man and woman with an almost unlimited capacity and opportunity for touching and loving each other. For it is useless to advise an act which most men find difficult — to touch his woman lovingly whenever she is near and at leisure. Almost any man will understand that when he is tired, he usually prefers not to be touched (before he learned the Tao of course) by his woman for two simple reasons: he is afraid he might not be able to satisfy her or he simply wants to go to sleep undisturbed. But when a man has learned how to regulate his emission he has no such fears and even when he wishes to go to sleep he can enjoy being touched and caressed to sleep. He might even make love a little (when you have learned the Tao, love-making is not strenuous any longer). And nearly any experienced woman will feel deeply that she seldom has enough loving/touching by her man. It is no exaggeration to say that this dissatisfaction drives many women to lesbianism[18] and many more women turn their affections to their pet animals, who as a rule will always respond warmly to touching. Frequently women confess that they turn to their own sex because they feel only another woman can understand deeply this need for caressing. This is not

[18] In Anais Nin's *Journal*, Vol. 2 and *The Lesbian Myth* by Bettie Wyson one could find evidence to substantiate this. In Nin's *Journal* there is a lesbian who clearly states that to be loved and touched by a man would be more ideal, turning to a woman is only her second choice.

26

always true of course. For by nature a man's need for loving/touching is just as great; the problem is that the overwhelming majority of men have never had an opportunity to learn adequately how to cope with the situation. An interesting example to explain this can be found in a man called Léautaud who is mentioned in this book.

When a man has learned the Tao he will enjoy infinitely more the loving/touching, for the reason that there is a very narrow boundary line between loving/touching and actually making love. But a man may not understand this completely until he has learned the Tao. A Tao of Loving adept not only enjoys much more, but he and his partner benefit from their loving as well. And we shall explain the reason in a moment.

6. *Nei tan (inner elixir) and wai tan (outer elixir)*

Having learned how to relax and be at peace with his environment, a Taoist usually enjoys his life greatly. As a result he seeks more actively a long, healthy life. No wonder that nearly all the great ancient Chinese physicians were Taoists. Also, because there have been so many Taoists over so many thousands of years, it is not surprising that there are many different approaches to longevity.

Basically there are two main schools — the school that advocates mainly the outer elixir and the school that mainly believes in inner elixir (we say 'mainly' here because the dividing line is not clearly defined). The 'outer elixir' Taoists were alchemists who were always in search of purifying potions that might lead them to immorality. The inner elixirists were more realistic and more prudent: they believed that what is inside oneself is safer and is enough to prolong one's life. A convincing example can be found in the famous physician Sun S'sù-Mo, who lived more than one century, from A.D. 581–682, and was a strong advocate of inner elixir and avoided all medicines unless all natural methods had failed.

We will not go into the details of the outer elixir, which relates to the purifying of compounds and metals into golden tablets. But we shall take a closer look at the inner elixir of which the Tao of Loving constitutes the most important part.

The inner elixir is mainly to do with the mind. For example, we achieve ejaculation control mainly through the mind, and we learn how to breathe correctly also mainly through the mind. But of course not only the mind. What the inner elixirist tries to achieve is as nearly as possible a perfect co-ordination of one's body and soul. He accomplishes this through a regimen of exercises.

The second important factor in inner elixir is conserving or saving many things that scientifically-minded people might deride. But personally I do not. As time passes, one after another of the seemingly ridiculous things they were doing turns out to be sensible. Later we shall discuss a man's semen, but another recent interesting example is the saving of one's sweat. For years the Western physiologists have advocated the healthy effect of exercising to the point of sweating, but anyone who has read the popular book called *Total Fitness* by L.E. Morehouse may have second thoughts. Morehouse is perhaps the first Western physiologist to advocate that one should save one's sweat. He believes that when a person sweats that is when he has already exercised too hard. And a Taoist would add that copious perspiration is a sure sign that the person has not learned to relax enough. We shall not dwell too long on the subject of inner and outer elixirs but if you wish to understand it in greater depth you could find all you want to know in Joseph Needham's *Chemistry and Chemical Technology*, Vol. 5 of *Science and Civilisation in China*, Part 5; 'The outer and inner Macrobiogens; the Elixir and the Enchyinoma'.

Chapter Two

Understanding
The Tao of Loving

*. . . no medicine or food or spiritual salvation
can prolong a man's life if he neither
understands nor practises the Tao of Loving.*
P'ÊNG TSU

1. Three basic concepts of the Tao

THERE ARE THREE BASIC CONCEPTS THAT DISTINGUISH THE TAO OF LOVING from other sex studies. These must be understood properly before they can be mastered. (A fuller discussion of these concepts follows on pp.32, 35–46, 70–71.)

The first concept is that a man must learn to find the right interval of ejaculation to suit his age and physical condition. This should strengthen him so that he can make love whenever it suits his and his partner's wish, and to continue a love-making for as long (or resume it as often) as it takes his partner to reach complete satisfaction.

The second concept involves a revolution in Western thinking about sex. The ancient Chinese believed that ejaculation — especially uncontrolled ejaculation — was not the most ecstatic moment for the man. Once he knows this, a man can discover other much more delightful joys in sex. This, in turn, will make it easier for him to control the emission of semen. This second concept is a direct derivation from the dialogue between Tsai Nü and P'êng Tsu quoted in *Ejaculation Reconsidered* (see pp.21–2).

The third concept — very significant in a different way — is the importance of female satisfaction. This has already been well publicized in the West through the work of Kinsey and successive Western sex researchers. Their results have been given still wider currency in recent years by the various Women's Movements and the validity of their conclusions is hardly in doubt any longer.

These three concepts are the real basis of the ancient Chinese philosophy of loving. They not only enabled men and women to come close to making love for as long and as often as they wanted, but also they gave ancient China a sexual freedom and naturalness which flourished so long as Taoism remained dominant. The Taoists held that sexual harmony put one in communion with the infinite force of nature, which they believed had sexual overtones too. Earth for instance was the female, or Yin element, and Heaven the male, or Yang. It was the interaction between these two that constituted the whole. By extension the union of men and women also created a unity. And one was as important as the other.

2. *The role of women*

From the very beginning women played a significant role in the philosophy of the Tao of Loving. They were prominent as Tao of Loving masters and advisors to the Emperor. It was not until much later in Chinese history that women's role degenerated into a subordinate one. The importance of the woman's place is amply illustrated in the Tao of Loving texts, some of which are still available to us. Many of these are written in the form of dialogues. Among these are the dialogues of Emperor Huang Ti and his female advisor, Su Nü. As we have already seen in dialogues quoted above, their language is charming and descriptive. For instance, 'phallus' becomes 'jade stem' (*yü hêng*) and 'vulva' the 'jade gate' (*yü mên*). An interesting point in relation to this is that the ancient Chinese never used terms as pejoratives the way people often use them today. Their open and uninhibited attitude towards sex made it impossible for them to think of sexual terms as 'dirty words'. In this book we sometimes use the ancient *yü hêng* in place of 'phallus' for the sake of variety.

3. *Importance of love-making*

How important love-making was to the ancient Taoists can be seen in this dialogue from the *Su Nü Ching*:

Emperor Huang Ti: 'I am weary and in disharmony. I am sad and apprehensive. What shall I do about this?'
Su Nü: 'All debility of man must be attributed to the faulty ways of loving. Woman is stronger in sex and constitution than man, as water is stronger than fire. Those who know the Tao of Loving are like good cooks who know how to blend the five flavours into a tasty dish. Those who know the Tao of Loving and harmonize the Yin [female] and Yang [male] are able to blend the five joys into a heavenly pleasure; those who do not know the Tao of Loving will die before their time, without even really having enjoyed the pleasure of loving. Is this not what your Majesty should be looking into?'

The dialogue continues with Huang Ti deciding to check this advice. He turns to another of his female advisors (he has four, only one of whom is male), Hsüan Nü:

Huang Ti: 'Su Nü has taught me how to achieve the harmony of Yin and Yang. Now I wish to hear what you have to say about the subject to confirm what I have learned.'
Hsüan Nü: 'In our universe all lives are created through the harmony of Yin and Yang. When Yang has the harmony of Yin all his problems will be solved and when Yin has the harmony of Yang all obstacles on her way will vanish. One Yin and one Yang must constantly assist one another. And thus the man will feel firm and strong. The woman will then be ready to receive him into her. The two will thus be in communion and their secretions will nurture each other . . .'

4. *How to observe female satisfaction*

Once Huang Ti accepted the advice of his advisors, he set about finding out in detail how to master the third principle of the Tao of Loving. He turned again to his chief female advisor, and asked:

Huang Ti: 'How does a man observe his woman's desires and satisfaction?'
Su Nü: 'There are ten indications. A man must observe and know what should be done. The ten indications are:

(1) Her jade hands holds his back, the lower part of her body moving. She sticks her tongue out licking him, trying to arouse him. This indicates that she is greatly aroused.

(2) Her fragrant body is supine and all her limbs are straight and not moving and she is breathing hard through her nose. This indicates that she desires him to resume his thrusts.

(3) She opens her palms to play with the sleeping man's jade hammer and turns it around. This indicates that she is hungry for him.

(4) Her eyes and brows are flickering and her voice utters gutteral sounds or playful words. This indicates that she is greatly aroused.

(5) She uses her two hands to hold her feet and opens her jade gate wide. This indicates that she is enjoying it greatly.

(6) Her tongue sticks out as if half-asleep or half-drunk. This indicates that her vulva is anxious for deep and shallow thrusts and she wants them to be done vigorously.

(7) She stretches her feet and toes and tries to retain his jade hammer inside her but she is not certain in what manner she wishes him to thrust. At the same time she murmurs in a low voice. This indicates that the tide of Yin is coming.

(8) Suddenly she has what she wants and she turns her waist a little. She perspires slightly and at the same time smiles. This indicates that she does not yet want him to finish because she still wants more.

(9) The sweet feeling is already there and her pleasure is mounting. Her tide of Yin has arrived. She still holds him tightly. This indicates she is not yet completely satisfied.

(10) Her body is hot and damp with perspiration. Her hands and feet relaxed. This indicates she is now thoroughly satiated.

There can be no doubt from the minute detail with which these indications are described that the Taoist physicians studied the matter intensively and there are signs that, for the purposes of scientific observation, a third person must have been present to note the woman's reaction during each stage of intercourse. It is also true that some love positions called for three participants and some information could have been obtained from these sessions.

5. *Misconceptions of the Tao*

For years the Tao of Loving has been imperfectly understood in the West. It has been misinterpreted by many Western writers, all of whom have given it names that never really seem to fit. A list of some of the more familiar would include these:

(a) *Coitus reservatus* is the term first coined in the West several hundred years ago. It is a misleading term because it focuses too narrowly on only one aspect of the Tao of Loving. For instance, among other things, it does not take into account the Tao's advice about regulated intervals of emission based on a man's age, strength and physical condition.

(b) *Male continence* is a term which originated at the Oneida Community, an experimental collective in Vermont, U.S.A. during the middle of the nineteenth century. It became more well known when it was mentioned by Havelock Ellis in his epoch-making book, *Studies in the Psychology of Sex*. As its name implies, male continence describes a way of loving which calls for the complete abstinence from emission except in cases when conception is desired. The Tao of Loving does not advise complete absence of emission except for the very old or the very sick.

(c) *Karezza* is a very passive form of love-making which was mistakenly identified with the ancient Chinese way of love in a particularly influential book of the 1920s, *Ideal Marriage*. The author, T.H. van de Velde, attacked this technique which had been popularized earlier in the century by Marie Stopes in her book, *Married Love*. In fact, Karezza bears very little resemblance to the Tao of Loving except where the latter applies to the very weak or the very old, who are advised to adopt a more passive method in order that they can still benefit somewhat from the communion of Yin and Yang. But the Tao certainly does not advise the young or the hale and hearty to be passive. Rather than the Tao of Loving, Karezza, as promulgated by Marie Stopes, more closely resembles male continence. It involves caressing and then a very quiet and passive coition without emission.

(d) *The mysticism of coitus reservatus* was a term coined by the late Dutch diplomat R.H. van Gulik in his admirable and detailed book in English (with certain passages in Latin) called *Sexual Life in Ancient China*, mentioned earlier. It is probably the only Western book which discusses the Tao of Loving at any length. Unfortunately van Gulik did not wholly understand the subject. He frankly admits this in the Preface to his book and this is why he uses the term 'Mysticism of Coitus Reservatus'. He explains further that as he did not understand the matter completely he was merely a compiler and he felt it his duty to transmit the rare and precious information he had gathered.

(e) *Tantric arts or Tantrism* is also often mistaken for the Tao of Loving. While Tantrism was influenced by, or may even have had its origins in the Tao of Loving, its various schools have developed into something quite different. The Buddhist Vajrayanic school mentions that China is the origin of its doctrine which is called 'the Chinese discipline'. The Indian way of loving is extremely ritualistic and more closely tied to their religion, while the Chinese Tao of Loving remained an important branch of Chinese medicine.

(f) *Imsák* (or *Ismák*) is something which we know little about. It seems to bear some similarities to the Tao of Loving. According to Sir Richard Burton, the *Ananga Ranga*, which he translated, states: 'This practice is called in Arabian medicine, *Imsák*, which means "holding" or "retaining".' Besides this brief description, there is little more we can say about *Imsák* because no book has ever been written about it. According to the late Aly Khan's biographer, Leonard Slater, Aly Khan practised the secret method of *Imsák*. Mr Slater describes the method as having originated many centuries before in the East. (The Arabs occupied parts of India for centuries from the eighth century and they could have adopted the Tantric practices. Or it is certainly possible that they learned directly from the Chinese during the same period.) By mastering *Imsák*, Aly Khan was able to control himself indefinitely and no matter how often he made love he did not emit more often than *twice weekly*.

Obviously, all these practices contain an element which is either derived from or similar to the Tao of Loving. But they are not the same thing. In the past, Western manners and Western preconceptions have hindered a proper understanding of the Tao of Loving. The Taoist concepts seemed too strange to be comprehended. During the last twenty years, however, attitudes in the West to love and sex have changed considerably.

Nowadays, we can easily accept the Freudian concept that mental health is closely tied to a satisfactory sex life and no neurosis arises without sexual conflict[1] — an idea first promulgated many thousands of years ago by Tao of Loving masters. In such a congenial climate it is perhaps time that the ancient Taoist philosophy of loving be fully explained.

[1]   Paul A. Robinson, *The Freudian Left*, p.14.

34

Chapter Three

Ejaculation Control

The male belongs to Yang
Yang's peculiarity is that he is easily aroused
But also he easily retreats.
The female belongs to Yin.
Yin's peculiarity is that she is slow to be aroused
But also slow to be satiated.

WU HSIEN

IN THE TAOIST SCHEME OF THINGS, MAN IS A YANG FORCE, AND HE HAS ALL the attributes of maleness. He is more volatile, more active and quicker than a woman, who has the attributes of Yin, the female force. She is more placid, her movements calmer — but ultimately she is stronger. A common analogy used in ancient texts when comparing the relative strength of men and women was to liken them to fire and water. Fire belongs to Yang and, though quick to ignite, it is overwhelmed by water, a Yin force. Taoist thought suggests that all forces occur in complementary pairs. Fire and water, heaven and earth, sun and moon, inhaling and exhaling, pushing and pulling, etc., and that each of these contrary forces[1] belongs to a sexual power — either Yin or Yang. Yin and Yang, although separate forces, are really part of the same ultimate unity and therefore necessary to one another.

Tao of Loving masters used those analogies when explaining physical sex as well. Wu Hsien (a Tao of Loving master during the Han Dynasty, 206 B.C.–A.D. 219) quoted above was noting what hundreds of sex researchers since his time have pointed out, if not as gracefully, always as forcefully. They all agree that men and women have different arousal times and different climax times and most sex partners nowadays are concerned to synchronize these times in order, literally, to 'come together'.

In *The Goals of Human Sexuality*, Irving Singer says: 'Very often women

---

[1] Pierre Teilhard de Chardin, *Towards the Future*, p.135.

hope to find a mate who will ejaculate at a time that coincides with their own orgasm; and for many men, as well, this kind of simultaneity signifies emotional oneness and a proof of mutual love. Frequently it does bespeak a harmony between two persons who attune their pleasure to each other's needs and inclinations. Certainly one can savour postorgasmic relaxation better if one's partner has been fully satisfied at approximately the same time.' [2]

Even in the West then ejaculation control is a very important part of love-making. It has always been perhaps the most important part of the Tao of Loving. The ancient Taoists gave great attention to every detail of control. An example of the advice they gave to novices can be seen in this passage from Wu Hsien:

(1) The beginner is advised not to get too excited or excessively passionate.

(2) The beginner should start with a woman who is not too attractive and whose jade gate [vulva] is not too tight. With such a woman it is easier for him to learn to control himself. If she is not too beautiful he will not lose his head and when her jade gate is not too tight, he will not get too excited.

(3) The beginner should learn how to enter soft and come out hard.

(4) He should first try the method of three shallow and one deep thrust and carry out the thrusts eighty-one times as one set.

(5) If he feels that he is becoming a little excited he should stop the thrusting motion immediately and withdraw his jade peak to a point so that only about one inch or more of it remains inside the jade gate [the locking method]. He should wait until he has calmed down and then resume thrusting with the same three shallow and one deep method.

(6) Next he can try the five shallow and one deep method.

(7) At last he can try nine shallow and one deep.

(8) In learning how to control ejaculation one must avoid being impatient.

Before we go on to give our own advice to novices let us look at some further words of Wu Hsien. Here, he gives a more detailed explanation of his advice so that the beginner has a clear understanding of not only what he should do but why he should do it:

(1) It is true that one must love one's partner in order to receive the greatest pleasure. But when you are learning and practising ejaculation control, you must make an effort and try to be indifferent so that you will be more composed.

(2) The beginner must thrust gently and slowly to carry out one set of thrusts, then two and then three sets. He could then stop for a while to recompose himself. A few moments later he could resume once again.

(3) In order to satisfy his partner, he must be kind and gentle so that she will reach

[2] Irving Singer, *The Goals of Human Sexuality*, p.50.

her orgasm quickly. But if he feels that he will soon lose control of himself he should withdraw somewhat his jade peak and apply the 'locking method'. Thus he will calm down once again and be able to resume his thrusts. For the beginner, thrusts must be carried out slowly and carefully.

Our own advice to beginners is not much different from this. Described in modern terms and with modern explanations it may sound somewhat different but basically the ancient Chinese gave sound advice.

A young man just starting his sex life should look for a woman who has some quality he really likes. The point is that, unlike an experience with a prostitute, he will want to concentrate on the woman as a person, to spend some time with her and to work for her satisfaction as well as his own. Young men – or men of any age, for that matter – ought to avoid prostitutes, but it is particularly important when they are learning ejaculation control.

There is, however, the danger that a woman may be *too* experienced. She may have developed a set pattern of love-making which 'satisfies' her. For instance, she may not be satisfied unless the man ejaculates. Many women have been conditioned to believe that unless a man ejaculates, he has not really been aroused. Scientists still argue over whether some women's demand for ejaculation is physiological or psychological. A woman who believes she must make a man ejaculate will go to some lengths to make him do so. Probably she will fellate him to make him do so quickly and very few men can resist the licking action of her tongue followed by her deep, soft sucking of his phallus.

For the ancient Taoists there was always an element of danger in fellatio, especially to the novices. While it was certainly regarded as an important part of foreplay – just as was cunnilingus – there was the ever-present danger of an uncontrolled ejaculation as the result. The Kronhausens made an interesting discovery in their research of Chinese erotic art: 'There are relatively few representations of fellatio; though a legitimate part of foreplay, it entailed the danger of man's ejaculation outside the vagina. Cunnilingus, however, is much more frequently represented, since it was traditionally considered an approved means of obtaining precious Yin essence from the woman.'[3]

1. *The true joy of loving*
The true joy of loving is an ecstasy of two bodies and souls mingling and

[3] Phyllis and Eberhard Kronhausen, *Erotic Art*, p.241.

uniting in poetry. Once a man has found an ideal partner he must try and make love to her ecstatically and poetically.

In an interview Masters once said he avoided using the word 'love' because it meant different things to different people and he did not want to get caught up in semantics. I am a devoted admirer of Masters and Johnson's research and books but on this point I do not agree with them entirely. Followers of the Tao of Loving feel that love and sex should not be separated. Love without sex is frustrating and unhealthy, lacking the essential harmony of Yin and Yang which brings peace and serenity to life. On the other hand sex without love is simply a biological function that does not bring us much closer to the mutual tranquillity we all need. In this book the word 'love' will be used as frequently as – or more frequently than – 'sex' in an attempt to correct the prevalent one-sided view of sex and orgasm.

Pure sex and orgasm may be joys but in our view they are not ecstatic joys which true mingling of love and sex can realize. For example, there are women who can achieve orgasm merely by crossing their legs and squeezing (and some can do so a dozen times a day). But by doing so, do they really achieve profound pleasure? Once a woman has a satisfying love experience, she rarely prefers masturbation. Masturbation is pure sex – without warmth, feeling, communication or the harmony of Yin and Yang. Equally, when a man makes love to a woman, he should not behave as if he is masturbating. Nothing frustrates or disappoints a woman as much as finding her love partner only cares about his own ejaculation. Love should be a true communion of the sexes. Instead of communicating tenderness and joy, sex for many men is simply a mechanical motion that is no different from masturbation, as though the woman did not exist. The result cannot fail to be a disappointment for all concerned. Some men may think they are satisfied. The fact is that they have never really known what true joyful loving is; nor do they realize that they have missed Yin/Yang harmony.

What then is true, joyful loving like? We can try to describe it as being like the joy of sitting under the blossom in a mountainous valley in May. Or swimming under the majestic waterfall of Lu Shan and facing the shimmering boundless lake Pu Yang, or listening to the chattering blue birds before the magnificent Grand Canyon in the golden setting sun after rain. What we are trying to say to young lovers is that they must try to cultivate and develop the capability of making love poetically and ecstatically. Once they have experienced this true joy of loving they will never settle for anything less and all petty and ugly thoughts will leave them for ever.

But how does a beginner begin? By exercising, opening up and sharpening all his senses and faculties — touching, tasting, seeing, hearing, talking and feeling. And by trying to use them all as fully as possible to give to and receive joy from his partner. He must learn that women no less than men like to be sincerely praised and appreciated especially while making love. In this way he learns not only how to make love ecstatically but also how to divert his mind from preoccupation with ejaculation.

Some sexologists suggest a kind of exaggerated nonchalance while making love to delay ejaculation. They advise men to think about politics or business while making love, or even to break off completely for a smoke. This may be an effective way to ward off ejaculation, but no way to achieve ecstasy or to even harmony with his partner who is sure to resent his remoteness or absent-mindedness — and with good reason. There are many more pleasant and joyful things for a man to think about — the texture of her hair, the smoothness of her skin, the mysteriously intriguing scent and curves of her body, her fragrant, moist lips and tongue and the even moister lips of her *yü mên.*

However, sooner or later a healthy young man is going to get to the crucial point when he wants to ejaculate. What, according to the Tao, should he then do?

For a young man between sixteen and eighteen, passing through the most fertile period in his life, it is supposed to be very difficult to control his ejaculation, but this is partly myth. There are some measures he can take if he feels ejaculation is imminent.

2. *The locking method*

The oldest and probably the best and simplest method is the one used by the ancient Chinese and described by Wu Hsien in this rather picturesque series of steps:

(1) The locking method is like trying to stop the Yellow River with one's hand. An impatient man will take more than twenty days of practice to learn it. A gentler person can learn it much faster, half the time is usually enough. Study the method carefully for about a month and then the man's precious treasure [semen, *ching*] will be quite safe.

(2) The advantage of the locking method is that it can be carried out simply. For example, when a man is doing the three shallow and one deep thrust pattern, he can close both his eyes and mouth and breathe deeply but gently through his nose so that

40

he will not start panting. When he feels slightly that he might soon lose control, he can lift his waist with just one quick movement and withdraw his jade peak one inch or more and stay in that position without moving. Then he can breathe deeply and diaphragmatically and at the same time contract his lower abdomen as though he is controlling himself when he is looking for a toilet. By thinking of the importance of treasuring his ching, and that it must not be lost indiscriminately, when he is deeply breathing, he will soon calm down. Then he can resume his thrusts again.

(3) The important point to remember is that he must retreat when he has just become excited. If he retreats when he is already very excited and tries to force his ching back, then the ching will not return, instead it will go into his bladder or even into his kidneys. If this happens, he may suffer from several diseases such as pain in the bladder and the small intestines or swelling and pain of the kidneys.

(4) To sum up, the locking method is excellent, but one must practise it when one is just beginning to feel excited. It is much better to retreat too early than too late. By practising this method, the man will be able to control his ejaculation rather comfortably without even letting his jade peak fall. He can thus save his energy and he will feel remarkably composed. And he should not emit his ching until he has completed at least five thousand thrusts. Combining the locking method with deep diaphragmatic breathing he could go on almost indefinitely. Then, to satisfy ten women in one evening would not be too difficult for him.

3. *The modern locking method*
Wu Hsien's locking method, translated into modern terms, is really very easy. When a man feels he is becoming too excited, he simply withdraws his penis for ten to thirty seconds. In this way, he wards off the danger of ejaculation and loses between 10 and 30 per cent of his erection. He can then re-enter and resume thrusting. He can do this as often as he wishes. As he gains experience, he will find that he needs to withdraw less and less often; eventually he should only need to do so on rare occasions.

The secret of success of the locking method is to recognize the approach of the point where you can no longer control ejaculation. Masters and Johnson call this the 'stage of ejaculation inevitability'. We call it more simply 'the point of no return'. Learning to recognize this point is vital — not just for ejaculation control, but in cases where both partners choose to rely on the withdrawal method of contraception.

4. *Masters and Johnson's squeeze technique*
In their book *Human Sexual Inadequacy*[4] Masters and Johnson suggest a 'squeeze technique' which was designed primarily to help premature ejaculators. For experienced lovers, it would be equally effective as a

---

[4] pp.102–7.

method of ejaculation control. We say 'for experienced lovers' because it is a rather elaborate technique and more difficult to learn than the Chinese 'squeeze technique' which we prefer. As pointed out above (p.20) the Masters and Johnson method can only be used if the woman is in the 'female superior' position. The man has to tell her when he is getting too excited. She reacts by quickly lifting herself off the penile shaft and using her fingers applies pressure on the coronal ridge area of his penis for three or four seconds. The pressure makes him lose his urge to ejaculate. He may also lose between 10 and 30 per cent of his erection. The woman must wait another fifteen to thirty seconds after she lets go of his penis before she reinserts it into her vagina and continues thrusting. She can go through this procedure several times in the course of one coition.

All this is fine for more experienced lovers. It is superb training for male/female communication-coordination during intercourse. But for the novice there are two main snags. First, the woman must know how to reinsert a partially soft phallus. Not so easy as it looks. If she fumbles, it may droop altogether and the erection may be completely lost. Second, the couple may not always be able to assume the female superior position. This position requires that the man reach and maintain a full erection securely. Many men have problems doing this.

5. *Ancient Chinese squeeze technique*
The ancient Chinese also prescribed a squeeze technique, or, more accurately, a pressuring technique. But it is much simpler than Masters and Johnson's. It can be used in nearly all positions. In this technique, the man himself applies the pressure. Using the fore and middle fingers of his left hand, he presses at the point between his scrotum and his anus for three to four seconds. At the same time he takes a deep breath. There are several advantages to this method. First, of course, the man does not have to withdraw his penis from the woman. Second, no time is lost in communication. Third, he does not have to say anything to his partner. Many men would prefer this technique just because they do not have to confide their problems.

6. *Advice for more experienced men*
Older men usually find ejaculation control much easier than young men. An older man's main problem is ridding himself of the idea that he must ejaculate every time he makes love. This may take some doing, after years of

conscious or unconscious conditioning. Once he has done it, however, he will find he can achieve a twenty-minute coition quite easily, with just a little practice. Be warned though: it will take a conscious effort on his part before he can rid himself of the ghost of 'ejaculation necessity'.

Perhaps instead of dwelling on the difficulty of learning ejaculation control, it would be better for the older man to look at some of the advantages. He will, of course, be able to make love more often and for much longer. He will find that his partner enjoys this much more too. Then he will be free to discover many pleasures — such as the special attributes of the woman that are lost in rapid sessions. He can discover her special smell and taste and texture; and more important perhaps is the special viscosity and smell and taste of her saliva, and of the natural lubricant from her vulva.

7. *Ejaculation frequency*

As a man grows older, the ratio of ejaculations to frequency of love-making should decrease. In other words, for the same number of coitions, there should be fewer ejaculations. He can make love as many times a day, or a week, as he wishes but he should not ejaculate more than once or twice a week if he is over fifty. This is true no matter how many times he makes love or how strong he is physically.

Tao of Loving masters placed particular emphasis on the retention of semen[5] and the regulation of ejaculation as the path to longevity. In a seventh-century book called *Longevity Principles* by Chang Chan, a number of theories are discussed. The yardstick for the regulation of ejaculation proposed by Tao of Loving Master Liu Ching is included:

In Spring, a man can permit himself to ejaculate once in three days. In Summer and Autumn, twice a month. During cold Winter one should save semen and not ejaculate at all. The way of Heaven is to accumulate Yang essence during Winter. A man will attain longevity if he follows this yardstick. One ejaculation in cold Winter is one hundred times more harmful than in Springtime.

[5] Although today many sexologists still hold the opinion that a man is able to replenish the semen 'inexhaustibly', this view must be interpreted with a little common sense. A simple way to explain this is to compare ejaculation with blood donation (physiologically the two are quite similar). To encourage the donors to feel free to give their precious blood the medical authorities usually say that a healthy human being is able to replenish his blood quickly and inexhaustibly. In practice, however, they do not as a rule encourage a donor to give blood more than once in several months, and often much less if the donor is not very strong or very young. Even with such precautions many people still experience tiredness or even fainting spells if they give blood frequently. Many men, the author included, have similar experiences when ejaculating too often. Because of this a great number of males do not dare to make love too frequently. But if a man has learned to regulate his ejaculations he can separate love-making from emission. As a result he can make love whenever he wishes to.

The preservation of Yang essence strengthened the Yang force in man and brought him closer to Heaven. It was important that he continuously nourished his Yang essence with Yin essence. This is why nearly all ancient Taoist texts stress the importance of making love frequently and ejaculating infrequently. The more one makes love, the more one benefits from the harmony of Yin and Yang; and the less one ejaculates, the less one loses the benefits of this harmony. In *The Secrets of the Jade Chamber* there is a dialogue between Emperor Huang Ti and Su Nü on this subject:

Huang Ti: 'I wish to hear the benefit of loving with infrequent ejaculation.'
Su Nü: 'When a man loves once without losing his semen, he will strengthen his body. If he loves twice without losing it, his hearing and his vision will be more acute. If thrice, all diseases may disappear. If four times, he will have peace of his soul. If five times his heart and blood circulation will be revitalized. If six times, his loins will become strong. If seven times, his buttock and thighs may become more powerful. If eight times, his skin may become smooth. If nine times, he will reach longevity. If ten times, he will be like an immortal.'

Like many ancient Taoist texts, this is exaggerated and poetic. No one was expected to take it literally in ancient China. By exaggerating, the author hoped to drive home his message — that a man should save his semen by controlling his ejaculation.

8. *Individual variations*

There is no ideal frequency for everyone. Individuals differ in size, strength and in stamina. And these are all important factors in determining individual frequencies. There is, however, a way of determining the correct ejaculation frequency for each person. It is quite straightforward. If a man of fifty feels very tired after ejaculating once every three days, then he should reduce to once a week. If he finds even this tiring and it takes him some time to recover his strength after his weekly ejaculation, he should wait even longer between ejaculations. He should know the right frequency by the fact that he will feel elated and happy after ejaculating. It will make him feel stronger instead of weaker, and more like a soaring hawk than a canary in a cage. And remember, no matter how often he ejaculates, he should try to make love daily — if possible, two or three times a day. He can forget about the old wives' tales that say love-making is harmful to older men. Unless his doctor has given him some sound medical reason for abstaining, then the more often he makes love, the more both he and his partner will benefit from the harmony of Yin and Yang.

9. *Not enough ejaculation*

Of course, a man might go too far the other way and not ejaculate often enough. Again, it is a matter of common sense. When he is learning ejaculation control almost every man will feel some discomfort or pressure in his scrotum. This may be imaginary and if he ejaculates once every three coitions and still feels uncomfortable, then probably it is. On the other hand, if he makes love once or twice a day for a week without ejaculating and feels some pressure, it is high time he allowed ejaculation to occur. Very occasionally tiredness or lassitude may be symptoms of ejaculating too little rather than too much. If either of these two signs occurs after he has not ejaculated for several weeks, he should try to increase his ejaculation frequency a little.

No one should allow himself to become a slave to a particular ejaculation frequency, and stick to it rigidly. Frequency depends on outside factors too. If a man has to work particularly hard one week, he may want to ejaculate less. If he is relaxing on holiday, he may want to ejaculate more.

There is no need to worry if you feel a pressure in your testicles in the early stages of learning ejaculation control. Too many men take fright at this and give up the struggle. Ejaculation control is a skill like any other and it takes practice to become proficient. Once mastered thoroughly, the body will adapt to it and it will become the most natural thing in the world.

10. *Premature ejaculation?*

This is a confusing term for a common complaint, yet, whatever it is, the Tao of Loving can easily solve it. The locking method or the squeeze technique will be useful in gaining control.

There has been a great deal written on the subject of premature ejaculation. All popular sex studies have done their research and come up with their standards of who is or who is not a 'premature ejaculator'. Kinsey, for instance, thought that anyone who could not keep his penis inside his partner's vagina for more than two minutes without having an orgasm was a premature ejaculator.[6] Masters and Johnson consider a man a premature ejaculator 'if he cannot control his ejaculatory process for a sufficient length of time during intravaginal containment to satisfy his partner in at least fifty per cent of their coital connections.'[7] In other words, if the female feels satisfied less than half the time her partner does, then that man is a

---

[6] Pomeroy and Martin Kinsey, *Sexual Behaviour in the Human Male*, p.530.
[7] Masters and Johnson, *Human Sexual Inadequacy*, p.92.

premature ejaculator. These figures however would not have been acceptable in ancient China. To the Tao of Loving masters any man who cannot wait until his partner has been thoroughly satisfied *every time* still has room for improvement.

It is obvious that 'premature ejaculation' is not a precise term and it should not be used indiscriminately. Nearly every young man starts his sex life with quick, uncontrolled ejaculations. He is excited, inexperienced and there is no one to guide him — especially if his partner is also a virgin. For the inexperienced man, making love with a young girl who has a tight vagina can make it very hard to control ejaculation.

Chapter Four

A Thousand Loving Thrusts

WHEN IT COMES TO EXPLAINING THE VARIATIONS OF STYLE AND DEPTH OF thrusting there is no greater Tao of Loving master than the seventh-century physician, Li T'ung Hsüan. His book the *T'ung Hsüan Tzu* deals in part with thrusting techniques. Of sixteen chapters, seven describe penile thrusts. The *T'ung Hsüan Tzu* identifies six styles:

(1) Make contact and press down the jade peak, shuttling back and forth, sawing the jade substance as though one is cutting open an oyster so that one may reach the sparkling pearls. This is the first style.

(2) Thrust down to the jade substance and pull up by the gold gully [the clitoris] as though slicing off stones to find beautiful jade. This is the second style.

(3) He uses his jade peak to thrust hard in the direction near the clitoris as if an iron pestle is pounding a medicine mortar. This is the third style.

(4) He moves his jade peak out and in, hammering at the left and the right sides of the 'examination hall' [sides of the vulva]. As if a blacksmith is shaping iron with his five hammers. This is the fourth style.

(5) He jabs his jade peak back and forth in short and slow thrusts inside the vulva, as if a farmer is preparing his land for late planting. This is the fifth style.

(6) The jade peak and the jade gate are grinding heavily and closely, as if two avalanches are mingling. This is the sixth style.

The Taoists devoted a great deal of time and study to the style and depth of thrusting, and not just because they enjoyed it. The reason was that, without a proper understanding of thrusting, there could be little benefit from the Yin and Yang communion. For the Taoists, coition was like trying to produce electricity. Without the proper friction, no spark could be obtained. Western scholars have overlooked the Taoist concern with correct thrusting. In *Ideal Marriage* van de Velde concluded that the Tao of Loving was a passive technique and compared it with the Karezza style of loving described by Marie Stopes. Nothing could be further from the truth.

Not only did the Tao recommend that these various styles of thrusts be vigorously employed, it also recommended a right number of thrusts in an ideal coition. Ancient literature often refers to 'a thousand loving thrusts' being necessary for a woman to be truly satisfied. Of course, such concern with numbers can be taken too literally, and 'a thousand loving thrusts' may sound more like hard labour than sexual pleasure to men who do not know the Tao of Loving. But for anybody who has mastered the Tao of Loving, it is not at all like hard work – quite the opposite.[1] There is a special pleasure for the man who knows he can give this degree of sexual satisfaction to his partner. The knowledge that he can satisfy the most voluptuous woman is enough to increase a man's confidence in himself.

When you look at what modern Western writers have to say about sex, the idea of 'a thousand loving thrusts' does seem revolutionary. For instance, David Reuben, in his popular book, *Everything You always Wanted to Know about Sex (But were Afraid to Ask),* advises: 'A reasonable yardstick for male potency is the ability to continue intercourse for five to ten minutes. During that time a normally potent male will deliver from fifty to one hundred pelvic thrusts.'[2]

And on the next page of the same book: 'Food and sex have much in common. In eating, the first bite is the tastiest, the first helping the most appetising. The third serving of strawberry shortcake just doesn't taste as good as the first time around. The third copulation of the evening is more for the record books than the enjoyment of the participants.'[3]

The first of these two excerpts is probably true for men who are unaware of the Tao of Loving. The second excerpt is more dubious. It certainly does not apply to any erotically awakened woman. Nor is it true for a man who knows the Tao. If a man has mastered the Tao of Loving and is truly fond of his partner, he will enjoy the third loving even more than the first. If we were to compare sex with food, like Dr Reuben, we would say the first copulation is the hors d'oeuvre; however tasty and succulent in itself, it only whets the appetite for the main course. When a man has mastered the Tao, he will find he wants a fourth or a fifth helping . . . In the words of the ancient Chinese, he'll feel 'as if he could never get enough of her'. And this is even more true for the woman.

1. *Male capacity can be greatly improved*
Prolonged intercourse not only greatly enhances the female partner's

---

[1] You can easily do it within half an hour or 1,800 seconds, a very slow rhythm indeed.
[2] David Reuben, *Everything You Always Wanted to Know about Sex (But were Afraid to Ask),* p.98.
[3] *Ibid.,* p.99.

48

pleasure, it is equally satisfying for the man. Of course, the length of time suggested by Havelock Ellis in his *Studies in the Psychology of Sex* (an hour and a quarter) and the number of thrusts proposed by Tao of Loving masters (a thousand) are only examples. No love-making session is so set and mechanical that it can be timed and measured. We are not advising that you should set the alarm clock or use a stop-watch every time you go to bed with someone. The figures simply suggest the sort of sexual capacity a man can reach with the help of the Tao. When a man has thoroughly learnt the Tao of Loving, he can easily make love for an hour and a quarter or even longer,[4] or with a thousand loving thrusts, if he can find a suitable partner for such an intensive session. Of course not all women are ready for such ardent love-making. And not all love partners are so attracted to each other that they want to make love for so long or so intensely. Even well-matched and highly-sexed couples do not want this kind of loving every day. Loving is at its best when it is at its most flexible. The important point to note is that a man may never again have to disappoint his partner or himself once he has mastered the Tao of Loving.

2. *Types of thrusts*

Thrusting in the Tao is very different from the standard Western method. In the right circumstances and with a congenial partner disciples of the Tao can thrust with amazing stamina and vigour. When partners are genuinely attracted to one another and know each other's bodies intimately, they can reach a degree of co-ordination that can seem incredible. A single coition can last a very long time and it can be repeated often and vigorously until both partners are completely satisfied. This is one reason why the Tao emphasizes different *types* of thrusts. If a man's phallus moves in and out of the vulva the same way every time, a long love-making session could become tedious. But when a man has learned how to vary his thrusting and positioning, a long session becomes a great advantage. And it is not an exaggeration to say that, up to a point, the more time he has, the easier for him to make the session into a memorable one.

The *T'ung Hsüan Tzu* contains a poetic description of what various thrusts should be like in a protracted session of love-making:

Deep and shallow, slow and swift, direct and slanting thrusts, are by no means all uniform and each has its own distinctive effect and characteristics. A slow thrust should resemble

---

[4] Havelock Ellis, *Studies in the Psychology of Sex*, Vol. II, Part 3, p.554.

the jerking movement of a carp toying with the hook; a swift thrust that of the flight of the birds against the wind. Inserting and withdrawing, moving upwards and downwards, from left to right, interspaced intervals or in quick succession, and all these should be co-ordinated. One should apply each at the most suitable time and not always stubbornly cling to only one style alone for reason of one's own laziness or convenience.

The book then described nine types of thrusts in detail:

(1) Strike out to the left and right as a brave warrior trying to break up the enemy ranks.

(2) Move up and down as a wild horse bucking through a stream.

(3) Pull out and push in as a group of seagulls playing on the waves.

(4) Use deep thrusts and shallow teasing strokes, alternating swiftly as a sparrow picking the leftovers of rice in a mortar.

(5) Make deep and shallow strokes in steady succession as a huge stone sinking into the sea.

(6) Push in slowly as a snake entering a hole to hibernate.

(7) Thrust swiftly as a frightened rat rushes into a hole.

(8) Poise, then strike like an eagle catching an elusive hare.

(9) Rise and then plunge low like a huge sailing boat braving the gale.

All these thrusts, when made at different speeds, intensities and depths, add shades and nuances of pleasure that will enhance the love-making of both men and women. Variation also provides the man with a method for controlling his ejaculation and keeping his phallus rigid for a suitable length of time.

3. *Depths of thrusts*

As well as types and styles of loving thrusts, the Tao of Loving also gives advice about the depth of thrusting. We turn once again to a dialogue between the Emperor Huang Ti and his female advisor, Su Nü. Here she describes the erotically and picturesquely named depths of the vagina:

Emperor Huang Ti: 'In male and female communion if one does not know how to regulate thrusting depth properly, one will not be able to reap the maximum benefit. I wish you could tell me the details of this.'

Su Nü: 'The man must observe what his woman's need is and at the same time treasure his ching [*semen* or essence] which he should never emit lightly. First he should rub both his palms to make them warm, and hold his jade stem firmly and next he should use the method of "shallow draw" and "deep thrust". The longer he can keep thrusting the more the partners will enjoy it. The thrust must neither be too fast nor too slow. Also he must not thrust too deeply without some restraint for he might injure his partner. Try several thrusts at "Lute String" and then vigorously some at "Water-chestnut Teeth". When the woman is reaching her peak of pleasure she will

unconsciously clench her teeth. She will perspire and her breathing will quicken. Her eyes will then be closed and her face will turn hot. Her organ opens wide and secretions are flooding. From this the man can see she is enjoying it very much. Also, Your Majesty should know that the depth of the vagina has eight names. They are called the eight valleys:

    (1) Lute String, the depth of which is one inch.
    (2) Water-chestnut Teeth, depth two inches.
    (3) Little Stream, depth three inches.
    (4) Black Pearl, depth four inches.
    (5) Valley's Proper, depth five inches.
    (6) Deep Chamber, depth six inches.
    (7) Inner Door, depth seven inches.
    (8) North Pole, depth eight inches.'

Emperor Huang Ti: 'And what is the method of nine shallow and one deep?'
Su Nü: 'That means simply to thrust nine times shallow and then once deep. Each thrust should be co-ordinated with one's breathing. The depth between Lute String and Black Pearl [one to four inches] is called shallow; between Little Stream and Valley Proper [three to five inches] is called deep. Thrusting too shallowly the couple may not feel the greatest pleasure, too deeply they may be injured.'

4. *Thrusting sequences*

Nine shallow and one deep seems a favoured method with nearly all ancient Tao of Loving masters and equally popular with women of all ages. From the point of view of the Tao, it is the best combination and the couple receive the maximum benefit. Women normally find it highly pleasurable. They feel tantalized, then satisfied.

There are many other thrusting sequences, such as three shallow and one deep; five shallow and one deep, etc. The reader can choose whichever combinations and variations suit him and his love partner best. The important thing to remember is that both partners should receive the most possible pleasure, and at the same time the man must remain in control so that he will not ejaculate too quickly or too often.

5. *Sexual gymnastics*

Western readers may be surprised by this emphasis on the number and type of loving thrusts. Only when they completely realize how important these are to the Tao of Loving technique, can they understand how seemingly impossible feats become not only possible but relatively easy. I was surprised myself when I first read the most famous Ming Dynasty erotic novel, *Jou P'u T'uan* ('The Prayer Mat of the Flesh'), many years ago. This was before I became fully acquainted with the Tao of Loving. One of the novel's heroines, Lady Blossom, says: 'You underestimate me. A man will have to shuttle back and forth between one and two thousand times before I begin to feel satisfaction.' I was incredulous. How could any woman need so much loving to be satisfied and how could any man ever live up to her expectations? Some years later however, after I had mastered the Tao, the two questions were answered automatically. Not only have I met women like Lady Blossom but also one thousand thrusts have become a relatively simple matter.

When you talk about numbers to do with loving, people may protest that you are talking like a sexual gymnast. But all types of gymnastics are becoming very popular these days. Most people now realize that without regular exercise they are going to grow old before their time. People are taking up jogging, weight-training and all sorts of body building activities. They have learned that this is the way to keep one's heart strong and circulation healthy. Half an hour's run is at least two thousand steps, so why sneer at one thousand or even five thousand loving thrusts? They are very similar, except that the latter are more interesting, far more mysterious and more pleasurable. And if your partner is a normal sensuous woman, she will enjoy your sexual gymnastics far more than she will your jogging.

6. *Master Sun's versatile methods*

Now let us look at a set of serene techniques proposed by a great master, some of which would be more suitable for the elderly, the less robust or the ill. It is this last part that may resemble slightly what van de Velde examined and wrongly concluded was the whole of the Tao of Loving instead of just one small part of it. Perhaps it fitted in with his preconceptions about the Chinese character. The Chinese are a prudent race and not noticeably adventurous; but at the same time, they are basically a vigorous and ingenious people. Both aspects of this heritage are incorporated into their ancient love theories. It should be noted, however, that Master Sun's versatile methods of applying Tao principles are a far cry from the truly passive and rigid (rigid in their attitude towards ejaculation) forms of loving called Karezza or male continence in the West.

Sun S'sû-Mo was born in A.D. 581 and lived for 101 years; he was a Taoist physician of great achievements[5] not only in theories of Tao of

---

[5] Sun S'sû-Mo invented inoculation for smallpox. He showed remarkable insight when he attributed tuberculosis to tiny creatures that ate away the lungs. He also divided tumours into five types, and developed treatment for all of them. When he was seventy-nine he was given the title Chen-jen ('Man of Wisdom') by the T'ang Emperor. After his long life he was called by people Jo Hwang ('King of Medicine').

Loving. He considered that if a man could make love one hundred times without an emission, he could live a very long life. His theory holds that when a man's *ching* (essence or semen) has become scarce, the man will become sick. Once the *ching* is exhausted, the man will die. Sun was obviously not a man of dogma. While he taught that one hundred coitions without emission was an ideal, he did not think that many men could achieve that goal. He therefore set down a somewhat simpler standard for the majority of men to follow: 'A man can also live a healthy and long life if he carries out a coition frequency of two emissions monthly or twenty-four yearly. If at the same time he also pays attention to wholesome food and exercises he may attain longevity.'

He then suggested yet another yardstick: 'A man of twenty can have one emission every four days. A man of thirty can have one emission in every eight days. A man of forty can have one emission in every ten days. A man of fifty can have one emission in every twenty days. A man of sixty should no longer emit. If he is exceptionally strong and healthy he can still have one emission monthly.'

Sun at no time suggested that strong, healthy men should refrain from emission completely as Karezza and male continence advise. In his writings he stated: 'When a man is unusually strong, too much suppression can be harmful. He will then suffer from pimples and boils if he does not emit for a long period.'

The only exception Sun S'sû-Mo made was for people who were extremely spiritual. Then he considered that complete abstinence from emission was perhaps advisable: 'When both partners are as spiritual as immortals, they can unite deeply without motion so that *ching* will not be stirred. At the same time the couple should imagine that there is a red ball as large as a hen's egg at their navels. They can thrust very lightly. But if they get excited they should retreat. In twenty-four hours the couple can practise this form of union dozens of times. By practising this they can also live a long time.'[6]

Sun S'sû-Mo never advocated that men and women should have no coitions at all. He warned against the harmfulness of living completely without the benefit of Yin/Yang harmony. The following dialogue appears in his book:

A Patient: 'When a man has not yet reached sixty years of age but is considering living

[6] This is very close to Marie Stopes's Karezza.

without the harmony of the opposite sex, do you think he should do that?'

Sun S'sû-Mo: 'No! A man cannot live long without a woman. A woman cannot live happily without a man. Without a woman he will long for a female all the time. This longing will tire his spirit. When his spirit is tired he cannot live long. Of course if he truly does not need or long for any woman that would be very good and he may also live a long life. But such a person is extremely rare. When one tries to suppress one's natural need to emit in a certain interval, it will be very hard to keep the *ching*, but very easy to lose it. He will lose it during his sleep or pollute his urine. Or he will suffer from the disease of mating with ghosts. When he loses his *ching* in such a manner it will be a hundred times more harmful.'

Chapter Five

Love Positions

ONCE A MAN HAS ACQUIRED THE ABILITY TO LOVE FOR HALF AN HOUR OR more at one time, frequent changes of position become extremely important. It is important that love-making loses none of its attractions through thoughtless repetitions and that partners do not become bored with one another. The communion of Yin and Yang must be joyfully maintained for the aim of good health, longevity and inner harmony.

1. *Four basic positions and twenty-six variations*
The ancient Chinese were very aware of this, and in his *T'ung Hsüan Tzu*, Master Li T'ung Hsüan describes not only the types and styles of loving thrusts, but also the range of love positions. He starts with the four basic positions:

(1) *Close Union*
(2) *Unicorn Horn*
(3) *Intimate Attachment*
(4) *Sunning Fish*

And then, in traditionally descriptive terms, he delineates the twenty-six main variations of these.[1]

(i) *Silkworm Spinning a Cocoon* (A variation on the first position) The woman, using both hands, clasps the man's neck and intertwines her feet across his back.

(ii) *Turning Dragon* (A variation on the first position) The man, using his left hand, pushes the woman's two feet up past her breasts. Using his right hand, he helps his jade stem into her jade gate.

(iii) *Two Fishes Side-by-Side* (A variation of the third position) Face-to-face and deep kissing, the man uses one hand to support the woman's feet.

(iv) *Loving Swallows* (A variation of the first position) The man is flat on the woman's abdomen. He holds her neck and she grasps his waist.

(v) *United Kingfishers* (A variation of the first position) The woman lies supine and relaxes her legs. The man kneels and holds her waist.

---

[1] We list the following picturesque names only for their historic interest and poetic charm. Readers are advised not to spend too much time trying to figure them out.

56

(vi) *Mandarin Ducks Entwined* (A variation of the fourth position) The woman lies on her side and curls her legs so that the man can enter from the rear.

(vii) *Flying Butterflies* (A variation of the second position)

(viii) *A Pair of Flying Ducks* (A variation of the second position) The man lies supine. The woman sits facing his feet.

(ix) *Dwarfed Pine Tree* (A variation of the first position) Woman crosses her legs entwining the man. They both hold each other on the waist with two hands.

(x) *Bamboos Near the Altar* (This variation does not belong to any of the four basic positions) Both the man and the woman stand face to face, embracing and kissing.

(xi) *Dance of the Two Phoenix* (A variation of the first position, but by turning it could also be a variation of the second position)

(xii) *Phoenix holding her Chicken* (This position is particularly suited to a couple of whom the woman is large and generously proportioned and the man is small)

(xiii) *Flying Seagulls* (A variation of the first position) The man stands at the side of the bed and holds the woman's legs while he enters her.

(xiv) *Leaping Wild Horses* (A variation of the first position) Her feet are on his shoulders. He can penetrate her deeply.

(xv) *Galloping Steed* (A variation of the first position) The woman lies in a supine position and the man squats. His left hand holds her neck and his right hand clasps her feet.

(xvi) *Horse's Hooves* (A variation of the first position) She lies supine. He puts one of her feet on his shoulder. The other foot dangles naturally.

(xvii) *Flying White Tiger* (A variation of the fourth position) The woman kneels with her face on the bed. He kneels behind her and has both hands holding her by the waist.

(xviii) *Dark Cicada Clings to a Branch* (A variation of the fourth position) She lies on her stomach and spreads her legs. He holds her shoulders and enters her from behind.

(xix) *Goat Facing a Tree* (A variation of the fourth position) The man sits on a chair. The woman sits on him with her back to his face, while he holds her by the waist.

(xx) *Wild Fowls* (A variation of the first position)

(xxi) *A Phoenix Plays in a Red Cave* (A variation of the first position) She lies supine and holds both her feet up in the air with her own hands.

(xxii) *A Giant Bird Soaring Over a Dark Sea* (A variation of the first position) The man supports her legs on his upper arms while his hands hold her waist.

(xxiii) *A Singing Monkey Holding a Tree* (A variation on the second position) The man sits as if on a chair. The woman sits in a riding manner on his lap face-to-face, holding on to him with both hands. He supports her with one hand on her buttocks and his other hand on the bed.

(xxiv) *Cat and Mice Share a Hole* (A variation of the second position) The man lies on his back and relaxes his feet. The woman lies on him closely. His jade stem achieves deep penetration.

(xxv) *Late Spring Donkey* (A variation of the fourth position) She supports herself on her hands and feet, bending over. He stands behind her, holding her waist.

(xxvi) *Autumn Dog* (A variation that does not belong to any of the four basic positions) The man and the woman are back to back, supporting themselves on their hands and feet and supporting each other with their buttocks. The man lowers his head and, lifting one hand, inserts his jade stem into her jade gate.

2. *Finding one's own positions*

No book can provide ideally suitable positions for all couples. The best a book can do is to give some good examples and then to instill into the readers the idea that they must constantly discover positions particularly suitable for them. As the students of Tao advance to longer and longer coitions, loving would become routine if there were no constant experimentation. Finding the most suitable position for both partners is vitally important. A man could not practise various styles and types of thrusting if either he or his partner was uncomfortable. It is a fallacy to think that a man and woman automatically fall into bed in the perfect position for both of them. The most experienced man and woman, making love together for the first time, may not hit it off perfectly. It can take ten or more encounters before they become used to one another's bodies — and even then, if they continue to experiment, they may discover still better and better positions. To the ancient Chinese, such constant searching for perfection in itself added zest and ecstasy to love-making.

The reason why a book cannot supply an individual couple with the most suitable position is simply because we are not built alike. No two couples come in exactly the same combination of shape, size, height and weight of their bodies or in placement, depth, width and length of their sex organs.

It is unfortunate that most popular sex manuals illustrate a number of picturesque love positions but neglect to stress that an individual couple must adapt them to their own needs in a versatile and imaginative way. Trying to imitate these colourfully drawn and eloquently named positions can only lead to confusion and embarrassment. Very few couples can copy the idealized couples in the instruction books. Forget about copying — find your own positions through your own experiments. At best, a book can only be a starting point.

Here then is a list of the four basic positions, and suggestions as to how you can discover your own variations.

The four basic positions are:

(1) Male superior
(2) Female superior
(3) Male and female face-to-face but side-by-side. The male on his right side, the

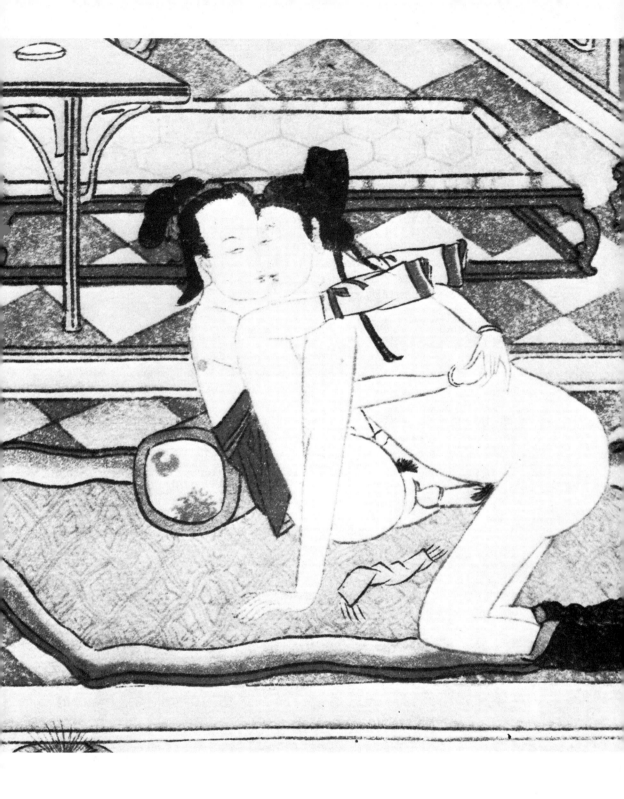

female on her left side or vice versa.

(4) Male entry from the back. This is the way most animals copulate. Human beings can do it quite comfortably in bed with both the male and female lying on their right or left sides or with the male lying on top of the female.

These positions have endless variations. One might be useful for a couple where the man is a head taller than his partner; another might suit a couple who are the same height. Other differences arise because some women have their vaginal opening situated much further forward than others. In fact, it is precisely these physical differences which make the number of positions literally infinite. For example, from the male superior position alone, we could deduce all these different postures:

(i) The male may support himself with his palms.

(ii) He may support himself with his elbows.

(iii) He may use his hands and arms to hold the lower part of his partner's hips.

(iv) He may hold her mid-hip.

(v) He may hold her waist.

(vi) He may hold her chest.

(vii) He may hold her shoulders — his left hand on the side of her right shoulder and his right hand on the front of her left shoulder.

(viii) He may support himself on his elbows with his arms about her back and shoulders so that their bodies are in close contact from head to toe. This is an interesting variation if the partners are about the same height. Each time the man makes a thrust, he pulls the woman's shoulders to gain momentum. This variation can give an ecstatic sensation that the partners are truly loving with their whole bodies and not just their sex organs. There are even variations on this variation, in the different ways the female holds her legs. She can either close her legs or open them or cross them on top of the man's body. This leads to even more variations in the way she crosses her legs — on his waist, below his hips and so on. The possibilities keep multiplying.

(ix) He may hold his partner very close.

(x) He may hold her at arm's length and use only hip movements for thrusting.

(xi) She may close her legs tight and straight.

(xii) She may open her legs wide. This is suitable for a woman with a relatively deep vagina and a man with an average-sized phallus.

(xiii) He holds her legs on his shoulders. This variation is for very deep penetration and can make some women extremely excited. Some women can stand only a few deep thrusts and some none at all because they have a very short vagina and it may hurt them. Some men like this variation because it gives them a peculiar sensation when their scrotum touches the woman's soft behind each time they make a deep thrust in this position.

This should give you some idea of man's — and woman's — 'infinite variety'. Above all, it should encourage you not to follow or be satisfied with suggestions like these, but to improvise and experiment with your love partner. You may come up with something much more suitable for your special body combination as well as your personal tastes and preferences.

3. *Changing positions*

A word about agility. When a man has become expert in prolonging the duration of his thrusts, he should learn to shift from one major position to another without interrupting the flow of intercourse. For instance, when he is in the male superior position he can, by tilting, transfer himself and his lover to the side-by-side position. Again, this is a basic position with limitless variations. Here is a particularly interesting one: the man holds his partner's right hip just below her waistline and pulls it to gain thrust momentum. At the same time she rests her right leg on his left arm. By using some ingenuity and originality you can contrive any number of variations from this one variation alone. For instance, by varying the ways in which the couple hold each other, by how near or how far away from each other they stay or by the way in which the woman parts her legs, and so on.

4. *Female superior position*

From the side-by-side position one could, with a quick, smooth roll, transfer to the female superior position. This can be most easily done on a wide bed or with a large mattress on the floor, but agile couples can manage it in even less space. It is very well worth practising because, as a manoeuvre, it has two special advantages. The first is that a shy or inexperienced woman may be reluctant to initiate the female superior position. Using the quick roll method she can be put easily and naturally into this position – without her bashfulness really entering into the decision. When she finds herself uppermost, she may decide she likes it very much indeed. Besides, there are sound physical reasons for this. Some women cannot reach orgasm in any other position. In the female superior position, the woman takes a much more active role and can select for herself the most exciting way and angle of thrusting. Previously non-orgasmic women have been known to achieve orgasm for the first time in this position.

5. *Advantages of female superior position*

The female superior position also has some advantages for the man, especially for older or less energetic men with young and vigorous female partners. From almost any variation of this position, the woman supplies nearly all the momentum of thrusting. The man can relax and enjoy himself. Furthermore, many men can control ejaculation far longer in this position.

Also, using the 'quick roll' method means the man does not have to withdraw his phallus in order to change positions. For a man who tends to lose his erection once his *yü hêng* leaves the warmth of the vagina, or once thrusting is interrupted, this can be a blessing.

6. *Variations in the female superior position*
There is a popular notion that the female superior position is one in which the woman mounts her partner as if she were riding a horse. This, of course, is only one variation and one many people enjoy. Another way would be for her to lie down full length on the man's stomach and kiss him on the lips while her legs are either wide open or held tightly together. This is a comfortable change from being on her knees all the time. She can gyrate in slow motion while her belly and breasts are in close contact with him. Or she can shake in quick, short thrusting motions like a fish caught in a net. Many women find this latter motion very erotic: strictly speaking it isn't a 'thrusting' motion as such since the phallus and the vulva remain closely and continuously in deep contact. This full-length lying down variation of the female superior position has one more advantage, that is, the man can fully appreciate the beauty of her beautiful hips, if she has them, with his hands and arms. And he should express his appreciation. From the popular 'riding' position, the woman can turn around completely, and facing the man's feet becomes another interesting and exciting variation.

Problems sometimes arise with the female superior position when the woman's vulva opening is too far behind, when she is too bulky, or when she is inexperienced. Then she may not be so lively or so active when on top. In any or all of these situations, the man can help by meeting her thrusts half way, or he could pull her down or push her up with his hands on her shoulders in order to start a thrusting motion. He could just as well rest his hands on her hips, either on the upper part near her waist or the lower part near her thighs, depending on her height and which is most comfortable for the man to be able to push and pull.

7. *Back entry*[2]
The fourth basic position — back entry — has just as many variations as the other three. Five of the most common are:

(1) The male and female lie side-by-side in bed.
(2) The man lies on top of the woman.

---

[2] It is important that readers do not confuse this position with anal intercourse which the Tao of Loving does not recommend for numerous reasons of hygiene.

(3) The woman kneels on the bed and the man stands on the floor.

(4) The man and woman sit together on a chair.

(5) The woman leans against any supporting object such as a piece of furniture, a tree or a wall and the man enters in a standing position.

The difficulty in each of these five is that if the woman is accustomed to clitoral orgasm she will need the help of either her own or her partner's fingers on her clitoris in order to reach her climax.

8. *Experimentation is the key*

The secret of successful love-making lies with the individual couple and their uninhibited will to experiment. Do not be taken aback by your partner's new ideas or suggestions. Making love in the same way all the time could be compared with eating bread and milk every meal every day. Very soon one would become very tired of the same unimaginative diet. It is no exaggeration to say that positioning is the spice of loving. Without its endless variations, loving would be much less of an ecstasy.

Chapter Six

Erotic Kissing
and The Tao

THERE IS A MYTH ABOUT THE CHINESE AND KISSING. MANY WESTERNERS firmly believe that the Chinese do not kiss. But this is far from the truth. The Chinese do not greet one another in the street with a peck on the mouth or cheek — the way the French and the Americans do — but that is hardly the kind of kissing we are talking about here. There is a world of difference between a fraternal buss on the cheek and a deep, passionate invitation to love by using one's mouth, lips and tongue without words.

Where and how the idea that the Chinese do not kiss got started is hard to say. Even van de Velde — a lifetime student of sexology — was under this misapprehension. In *Ideal Marriage*, he writes: 'Japanese, Chinese and Annamese do not kiss as we understand the term. Instead of mutual contact of the mouth, there is nasal contact, with delicate inhalation.'

Whatever may be true about the Japanese and the Annamese, we do know this is not the way the Chinese kiss. Van de Velde may have got his ideas from the Chinese custom of sniffing their babies in public. They are very fond of doing this and well-cared for babies do have a very sweet, special aroma of their own. It may well be that this was the only sort of 'kissing' he ever saw in public because, while it is true that the Chinese kiss, they consider it a very private action and it is rarely done in public places. In the West, where kissing, even very passionate kissing, is done in an uninhibited way these days, the Chinese may seem restrained. Perhaps they are. Nevertheless, the ancient Chinese took erotic kissing as seriously as an inalienable part of sexual communion.

1. *The Yin essence*

Tao of Loving Master Wu Hsien goes into great detail about erotic and passionate kissing in his essay 'The Libation of the Three Peaks'. These peaks produce essences which were very important to the harmony of Yin and Yang and the whole metaphysical structure of Taoism.

64

(1) The highest is called 'Red Lotus Peak' [lips]. Its libation 'Jade Spring' comes out from two holes under the woman's tongue. When a man licks it with his tongue it will rush out from its pool. It is transparent in appearance and greatly beneficial to man.

(2) The next is called 'Twin Peaks' [breasts]. Its libation 'White Snow' comes out from the woman's nipples. It is white in colour, sweet to taste. Drinking it is not only beneficial to the male, it will be even more so for the female. It will strengthen her blood circulation, regulate her periods. It will relax her body and soul to make her happy and at ease. It will affect the production of liquid in both her 'Flowery Pool' [mouth] and her 'Dark Gate' [vulva]. Of the three libations this is the most superior. If the female has never borne a child and produces no milk, the effect can be even better.

(3) The lowest is called 'Purple Mushroom Peak' or the 'White Tiger's Cave' or the 'Dark Gate' [vulva]. Its libation 'Moon Flower' is safely kept in her 'Palace of Yin' [womb]. The liquid is very lubricating. But the gate of the 'Palace of Yin' is nearly always closed. It opens only when the female is greatly pleased to the point that her face turns red and her voice is murmuring. Then the libation floods out. At that time his jade peak should retreat about one inch but continue his thrusts and at the same time either kiss her mouth or drink her nipples. These are what we call the libations of the three peaks. The one who knows the Tao sees but is not carried away by his passion. The couple is seemingly absorbed in lust. But that is no earthly lust and that is why they are able to benefit from it . . .

2. *Erotic kissing and oral sex*

Nearly all the ancient books on the Tao of Loving emphasize the importance of deep, erotic kissing. They place it second only to the actual act of coition. In erotic kissing, as in sexual intercourse, men and women benefit from the harmony of Yin and Yang. So long as both the man and woman enjoy it, they should kiss deeply as often as possible. And they should drink each other's fluid. The drinking of the 'jade fluid' – or saliva – is vital to the harmony of Yin and Yang. Cunnilingus and fellatio – or oral/genital kissing – are regarded as very effective ways of arousing a man or a woman. But there is a warning that a man must be careful not to let himself become so carried away that he gives in to uncontrolled ejaculation. To carry out successful fellatio a woman must learn to relax her mouth. If she is tense or stiff she will not be able to use her lips to shield her teeth and may hurt the *yü hêng* instead of libating it. Some women enjoy having their clitoris nipped, but men seldom, if ever, like to have their phallus bitten – however playfully.

Cunnilingus has almost no such drawbacks and is highly favoured by many women.

3. *Advantages of erotic kissing*

Learning how to kiss all parts of the body properly is a relatively simple but important matter. Simple, because there are no obstacles to overcome in kissing such as premature ejaculation, impotence or lack of lubrication. The only barrier is a psychological one. In many people's minds, a kiss is just a ritual smack: they do not distinguish between one kind and another. Yet there is a world of difference between a deep, inspired, erotic kiss and a boring antiseptic pressing together of lips. One can be earth-shaking, to the point that some women have an orgasm from such ecstatic kissing; while the other is barely noticeable. A passionate kiss can be a revelation and even more gratifying than a routine coition. It is, therefore, important to understand how to use your lips, tongue and mouth for mutual pleasure and benefit. As Havelock Ellis puts it: 'We have in the lips a highly sensitive frontier region between skin and mucous membrane, in many respects analogous to the vulvo-vaginal orifice and reinforcible, moreover, by the active movements of the still more highly sensitive tongue.'[1] In other words, in the lips and tongue we have erotic organs with the characteristics of *both* the vulva and the phallus. Nor have they any of the limitations which often handicap the vagina and the penis. Vagina and penis are, to a large extent, controlled by involuntary muscles, whereas our lips and tongue are controlled by voluntary muscles. This means we can kiss as much and for as long as we want — even when we are approaching exhaustion. We do not have the same control over our genitals. Even a man who has mastered the Tao of Loving would have a problem in achieving an erection if he was totally exhausted. And a man and a woman would have similar trouble making love in a prostrated state. Two terribly tired people can continue loving one another with their lips and tongue after their genitals have stopped functioning.

4. *Nipple kissing*

It is a widespread view that kissing a woman's nipples will as a rule prepare a woman for coition. In practice however it is not quite so, and reactions vary widely from woman to woman. While some women's breasts are nearly numb, others are so sensitive that fondling their nipples can bring them to orgasm. Whereas most women enjoy their breasts being sucked very much, there are still quite a few who dislike it. A man should try to find this out, for such sucking is highly beneficial to you both. Of course, you will

[1] *Studies in the Psychology of Sex*, Vol. I, Part 3, p.22.

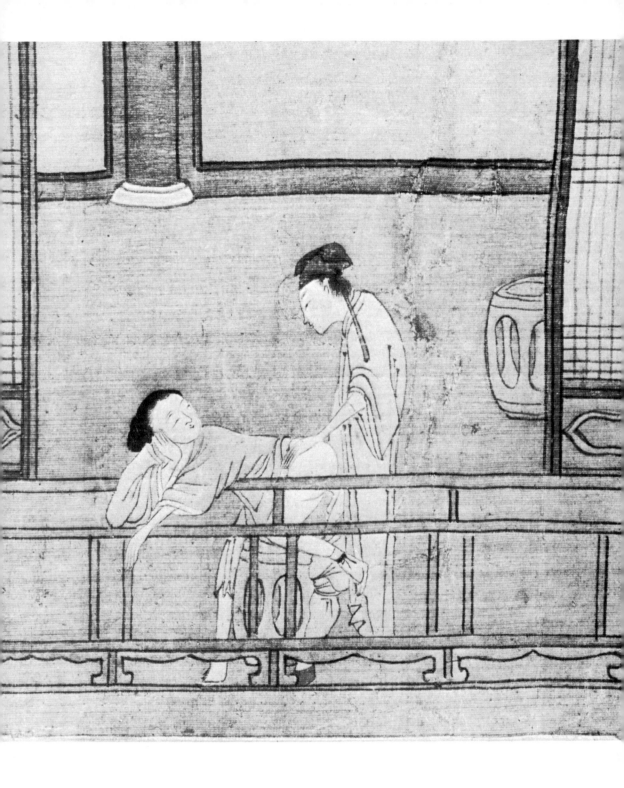

handle her breasts very gently. And you will soon realize that with many women there is a direct connection between nipples and vulva. Stimulating those two delicate buttons either by kissing, sucking or caressing will give many women great pleasure in the vulva and quickly result in the vagina overflowing with lubricant. Yet with many others there seems no such connection. Strange as it may seem, the size or beauty of a woman's breasts is irrelevant to whether she enjoys them being kissed, sucked or licked. If the man is patient and skilful enough however, this seeming lack of connection or sensitivity can often be awakened and activated in a matter of a few months by regular gentle sucking and caressing. The nerve connections are always there. They remain dormant only because of the absence of stimulation.

5. *Improving erotic kissing*

First the oral and facial muscles should be relaxed. Relaxation of the mouth and the tongue makes erotic kissing possible because only then you can enter into a rich, pleasurable contact with your partner's lips and tongue. A tight, tense mouth not only loses a great deal of its sensitivity, it also tends to fight against your partner's instead of fitting it closely. When this happens, a kiss loses much of its sensuality because of the poor contact and empty space it creates. Remember, the less empty space there is in your mouth when you are kissing deeply, the more blissful the pleasure will be.

Second, remember that erotic kissing involves nearly all the senses — touch, smell, taste, even hearing. For this reason you must pay scrupulous attention to your physical hygiene and health. Bad breath, for example, can often be unbearably offensive, and usually a sign of a disorder in your mouth, sinus or digestive system. You should get it properly cured instead of just covering it up superficially with mouth wash or deodorant. Pay special attention before making love to ensuring that you are perfectly clean. Pungent odours from spicy foods can be offensive, particularly when your partner has not eaten the same food. Similarly non-drinkers and non-smokers may find liquor and cigarette smells repellant.

All this is important because, during deep kissing, the partners should drink from each other's lips and tongue as much as possible. They can test each other this way too. If exchanging fluids is repulsive to either, then perhaps the couple are not as well matched as they thought and should seek more sympathetic partners because without uninhibited mutual relish of each other's fluid, satisfying erotic kissing is impossible. And without it an integral part of loving is lacking.

We have not mentioned teeth so far, but they too have a part to play in erotic kissing. From time to time you can nip your partner's lips or tongue, always very lightly though so as not to hurt. Only genuine masochists find pleasure in pain. Biting or nipping is really most effective on the ears, neck and shoulders. Many men and women find this highly exciting, especially during intercourse.

Chapter Seven

Evolution and Debasement of The Tao of Loving

1. *Emphasis on female satisfaction*

The Tao of Loving owes its existence largely to the ancient Chinese desire to satisfy women as well as men. When the Tao of Loving was first formulated — several thousand years ago — people understood this. The Tao was known at that time as the Tao of Yin and Yang Communion, a title that underlines the harmony of male and female.

For Yin and Yang to be in harmony, a man must satisfy his woman completely. Emphasis on this concept is seen in several dialogues between Huang Ti and his advisor, Su Nü, on how to interpret a woman's reactions in love-making. In this part of the dialogue, Su Nü describes a woman's five basic responses to a man's overtures:

(1) If she desires to have him the man can notice a change in the way she breathes.

(2) If she desires him to enter, her nostrils will be extended and her mouth open.

(3) If she desires the coming of the tide of Yin her body will be shaking and holding him tight.

(4) If she is anxious to have complete satisfaction her perspiration will be copious.

(5) If her desire is thoroughly satisfied her body will be stretched and her eyes closed as if in deep sleep.

The following are ten more detailed indications of a woman's response and how the man is expected to do all he can to please her. The ten indications are:

(a) She holds the man tight with both her hands. It indicates that she wishes closer body contact.

(b) She raises her legs. It indicates that she wishes closer friction of her clitoris.

(c) She extends her abdomen. It indicates that she wishes shallower thrusts.

(d) Her thighs are moving. It indicates that she is greatly pleased.

(e) She uses her feet like hooks to pull the man. It indicates that she wishes deeper thrusts.

(f) She crosses her legs over his back. It indicates that she is anxious for more.

(g) She is shaking from side to side. It indicates that she wishes deep thrusts on both the left and the right.

(h) She lifts her body pressing him. It indicates that she is enjoying it extremely.

(i) She relaxes her body. It indicates that the body and limbs are pacified.

(j) Her vulva is flooding. Her tide of Yin has come. The man can see for himself that his woman is happy.

Tao of Loving Master Wu Hsien writing during the Han Dynasty (206 B.C.– A.D. 219) also lists a set of indications of female arousal:

(i) She is panting and her voice is shaking uncontrollably.

(ii) She closes her eyes and her nostrils are widened and she is unable to speak.

(iii) She is staring at the man.

(iv) Her ears turn red and her face is flushing but the tip of her tongue turns slightly colder.

(v) Her hands are hot and her abdomen warm and at the same time her language becomes almost unintelligible.

(vi) Her expression looks as though she is bewitched and her body is soft as jelly and her limbs are droopy.

(vii) The saliva under her tongue has been sucked dry and her body is pressing the man.

(viii) The pulses of her vulva become noticeable and her secretions are flooding.

To this Wu Hsien adds a word of caution: 'All the above indications prove that she is greatly aroused. But the man must keep the situation in control and benefit from the communion without undue haste.'

Until very recently the idea that female satisfaction is important was revolutionary. And it has literally taken a 'sexual revolution' in the West to get it accepted. In ancient China, however, it was basic to the philosophy of Taoism. When the Tao of Loving was first formulated, Chinese society probably had only just changed from matriarchy to patriarchy. The position of women at that point was nearly equal to that of men. For instance, three out of four advisors to Huang Ti in that period were women. Perhaps this is why the earliest Tao of Loving texts stress the importance of mutual harmony and equality in sex relations.

2. *The Han Dynasty*

Many, many centuries later, during the Han Dynasty, this balance broke down. Man became more and more privileged — politically, socially and sexually — and female equality disappeared. By then the Tao of Loving was known by such names as:

The Tao of Yin

The Affair of Yin and Yang
The Technique of Yin and Yang
The Technique of the Inner Chamber

It is significant that then for the first time the word 'technique' came into use. From the original philosophical concept, the Tao of Loving had become debased into a *style* of love-making. Even the term 'Tao of Yin' was used in a different sense. There were several books written during this period by different authors and yet all called by the same name *The Tao of Yin*. At first glance it might have seemed as if they dealt with the Tao from the woman's point of view. In fact they were exclusively for men on how to use their women or 'Yin'. The male viewpoint was dominant. Women were subservient or merely regarded as the tools for men's pleasure. Like everything else, love-making was considered as being exclusively for the benefit of men and to flatter male vanity and the woman's role was to enhance the superior position of the man.

In practice, however, things were better than they looked. The ancient principles of the Tao survived the social corruption. Authors and masters continued to emphasize the importance of the female satisfaction. Without a woman's willing co-operation a man could not truly enjoy love-making. The Kronhausens make an interesting comment on this point in their research into Oriental erotica. They note the difference between Chinese and Japanese attitudes to the role of women in love-making:

Another interesting difference we noted in Chinese as compared with Japanese erotic pictures, which sheds a great deal of light on differing sex attitudes that underlie these pictorial representations, concerns the fact that in Chinese erotic art one finds not infrequently the man entreating the woman to have sexual intercourse with him. In contrast to this, female reticence or resistance is overcome in Japanese erotic art by male aggressiveness, sometimes to the point of forceful intercourse and rape is a very rare subject matter in Chinese erotica.[1]

Certainly, for the Chinese Taoists, a man could not benefit from love-making unless he and his partner were in harmony. None of the Tao of Yin manuscripts from the Han Dynasty have survived,[2] but a Tao of Loving master of the fourth century, Pao Pu Tzu (the great alchemist Ko Hung), wrote:

Best medicine and nourishment of the whole world cannot help you if you do not know and believe the Tao of Loving . . .

[1] Phyllis and Eberhard Kronhausen, *Erotic Art*, p.243.
[2] Between the thirteenth and fourteenth centuries the Mongols controlled China for eighty-eight years and they banned every book on Tao except *Tao Tê Ching*. This is an important reason why we have so few of the Tao of Loving books left to us. It was a long interruption.

Hsüan Nü and Su Nü [two of Emperor Huang Ti's female advisors] of the ancient time compared communion of man and woman as fire and water. Water and fire both kill, but can also give life. It all depends on if one really knows the Tao. If he knows the Tao, then the more women he makes love with the better for his health. But if he does not know the Tao, then just one woman is enough to hasten him to his grave.

3. *From Sui to Ming Dynasty*

During the next or third period which began with the Sui Dynasty (A.D. 589–618) and continued until the end of the Ming Dynasty (A.D. 1368–1643) true harmony and co-operation between men and women broke down completely. The mutual caring of Huang Ti's time gave way to something close to superstition under those later Emperors. Men were taught to distrust and fear women. The Tao of Loving itself became corrupt. Chung Ho Tzu, a sixth-century Tao of Loving master, wrote:

If a man wishes to nurture his Yang essence he must *not* let his woman know about his technique. If he carelessly lets his woman into the secret, his technique will become not only useless it will become harmful to himself. It is very much like letting your enemy get hold of your own deadly weapon.

Another passage deals with an example of what evil can befall a man who gets into the hands of the wrong woman:

It is not only that a man could nurture his Yang by taking Yin essence from the woman. A woman could also take Yang essence from the man to nurture her Yin. The Queen Mother of the West[3] was such a woman, when she made love to a man he would immediately afterwards become sick while she kept herself youthful and handsome without powder or rouge. It is said that she adopted a diet of milk and cheese, and she was fond of playing the five-stringed lute to keep her heart and thoughts harmonious. It is also said that the Queen Mother had no husband but was fond of making love to young men. Her life is not a good example; even though she had the high position of a queen mother she should not have done so.

4. *Superstitions and vampirism*

This is just one of the several superstitions which developed many years after the first appearance of the Tao of Loving. Personally, I have never kept my own Tao of Loving practice a secret from my partner, and I believe, as did the ancient Chinese, that both partners should understand the subject properly in order to get the best results. The Queen Mother in this somewhat apocryphal story has all the characteristics of a vampire. The older woman craving the companionship of young men; the almost supernatural ability to remain young without the use of cosmetics; the Queen Mother's

---

[3] Hsi Wang Mu. Actually an ancient goddess, worshipped in the Han period.

tranquillity despite the death and destruction she causes fits in with the myth, common to all cultures, of the *femme fatale*.

Vampirism is a Western term. In art, the Norwegian painter Edward Munch has illustrated it in both lithograph and oils. He has several works entitled 'Vampire'. They are almost identical. All show a young woman kissing a young man on the back of his neck. The impression is of a vampire sucking the young man's blood. Throughout his life Munch was reluctant to get close to women: he thought that making love to a woman was a mating with death. His morbid fear of women was reinforced when his brother Andreas died in 1895 when he was still young and after having been married for only six months. Munch thought his sister-in-law was a good woman but too active and energetic for his brother.

In some ways, the ancient Chinese view of sexual relationships was close to Munch's. They too thought sex could be deadly for the man. But what they did about it was very different. Instead of retreating into themselves and into a morbid obsession the Chinese formulated the Tao of Loving. The Tao makes intercourse not only harmless for the man but positively beneficial for both parties. Just as man has learned to control and tame wild rivers and harness them for the benefit of mankind, so the Taoist masters regulated sex for the benefit of mankind.

5. *Some confusing notions*

According to the Tao, the only time love-making could harm a woman — whatever her age — was if her lover was inexperienced and left her perpetually unsatisfied. This is why the Tao of Loving stressed female satisfaction as one of its cardinal principles. However, it warned repeatedly that a man could be in a perilous situation if his woman persistently urged him to ejaculate. The most important part of the theory, ejaculation control, developed out of the attempt to reconcile female satisfaction and male well-being.

We can only guess how the notion that woman is man's worst enemy originated. It may have come from the first Tao of Loving book, *Su Nü Ching*. In it, Su Nü uses the term 'enemy' when she is making the point that man must treasure his *ching* (semen):

When a man is facing an enemy he should consider his enemy as a tile or a stone and himself as precious as gold or jade. As soon as he feels that he will lose control of his ching he should withdraw instantly. Making love to a woman is like riding a galloping horse with a rotten rein. Or as dangerous as walking on the edge of a deep pit that is

74

full of spikes. If a man can learn to treasure his ching he is quite safe with a woman.

It is a picturesque and effective warning to a young man, but it is open to debate what Su Nü meant when she wrote about an 'enemy'. My own opinion is that her words have been taken out of context, her meaning distorted. Her intention was not to condemn women as the 'enemy' but rather to encourage men to treasure their *ching*. To do this she used all sorts of metaphors and similes — the horse, the gold and jade, the pit with spikes, etc., as well as the word 'enemy'. Later some writers on the Tao of Loving seized on this passage to prove their own point about women and distorted the meaning. It is not likely that Su Nü could have been so disloyal to her own sex.

Another confusing notion which grew up around the Tao of Loving and became even more widespread was the idea of making love to as many women as possible in one night. Many later writers especially recommend this. This may have been inherited from the ancient polygamous Chinese society. Given this, and that a man who has mastered the Tao of Loving is quite capable of satisfying a great many women in one night, why not make love to the whole harem?

None of Huang Ti's three women advisors ever suggested he make love to many women in one night. At least not in any of the written dialogues which have come down to us. Only his male advisor, P'êng Tsu, made such a suggestion.

From the Sui Dynasty onwards women's position in China continued to deteriorate. In the T'ang Dynasty (A.D. 618–906), for instance, Taoism as a philosophy became very popular and the Tao of Loving along with it. Yet directly after this period the degrading custom of binding women's feet was introduced. Women were playthings — toys for men to use and discard. As a result the Tao of Loving was steadily corrupted and became known by several different names — all of which reflected a new and different emphasis from the original Tao of Loving:

The Chamber Technique
The Tao of Communion
Communion
The Method of Loving
The Battle of the Inner Chamber
The Battle of Yin and Yang.

The old idea of harmony and mutual benefit arising directly from the Taoist philosophy had been lost, love had become a battleground. Because of this some Western scholars such as van Gulik have deduced an element of vampirism in the Tao. And one can see why. Studying the Tao of Loving writers of this period would give this impression. Chung Ho Tzu, for example, corrupted the original concept of the early Tao of Loving — the harmony of Yin and Yang — in order to put across his own view of 'the battle of the sexes'. It was not until the eminent English scholar Joseph Needham probed into early Taoism and developed his own more accurate conclusions that van Gulik changed his mind on this point.

6. *How the Tao of Loving almost disappeared*

Taoism and the Tao of Loving went steadily downhill from the early Sui period with the exception of perhaps the early T'ang Dynasty. During the Ch'ing or Manchu Dynasty, it all but disappeared. The Manchus were a foreign ruling house in China and they feared the independent spirit of the Taoists. They suppressed them ruthlessly. The ideas of equality for women and of female sexual satisfaction were lost.

7. *The age of agony and frustration*

If we wish to coin a new term for our own age, we may fittingly call it 'The Age of Agony and Frustration': the agony and frustration of dissatisfaction in loving. Already in the academic research of sexologists like Masters and Johnson and in the popular works of writers like Kate Millett (*Sexual Politics*) and Norman Mailer (*The Prisoner of Sex*), we have uncovered the basic facts about women's sexual needs. It is no longer a forbidden subject. Ever since Havelock Ellis first suggested, early in this century, that all might not be well in our marriage bed, nearly everywhere the theme of female dissatisfaction has been fundamental to modern sexual enlightenment. Kinsey was the first to quote statistics. His research found that even supposedly happily married couples lived on a very slim diet of love. It was Kinsey who found that for three quarters of all men in the U.S.A. love-making lasts two minutes or less. And Masters has remarked more recently that with some married couples making love is as occasional as 'Sunday silver'. Love-making of this sort can never satisfy the needs of women. There has to be a better way. The Tao of Loving could easily provide the answer. A man who has mastered the Tao can fully and completely satisfy his partner without fail.[4]   In turn, he will find his own erotic pleasure tremendously enhanced.   He will be able to see and feel his woman's satisfaction, which is a great pleasure in itself; as well as that, they will both benefit from the harmony of Yin and Yang.

Some people may feel that all this is a waste of time and effort. Most likely these same people would not think twice about spending hours at a cocktail party or a whole evening over an elaborate dinner. Compare the pleasure you get out of each of these activities and you will see we have got our priorities wrong. If we could learn from the Tao and shift a little of our attention away from eating and drinking and on to loving, we might all be happier and healthier.

---

[4] See Havelock Ellis, *Studies in the Psychology of Sex*, Vol. II, Part 3, p.553. In a chapter called 'Art of Love', Ellis commented on the Tao of Loving which he called *Coitus Reservatus*: 'So far from being injurious to the woman, it is probably the form of coitus which gives her the maximum of gratification and relief . . . it is, however, a desirable condition for completely adequate coitus, and in the East this is fully recognized and the attitude carefully cultivated.'

Chapter Eight

The Conquest of Impotence

AT ONE TIME OR ANOTHER, MOST MEN SUFFER FROM TEMPORARY impotence. That is probably putting it too strongly. What we mean is that at one time or another most men think that they want to make love only to find that the body is not willing. We learn from *The Secrets of the Jade Chamber* that even Emperor Huang Ti had such painful moments. In a dialogue with Su Nü he describes his predicament and asks her advice:

Huang Ti: 'I desire coition but my *yü hêng* will not rise. I feel so embarrassed that my perspiration comes out like pearls. In my heart I crave to copulate and I wish I could help with my hand. How can I help? I wish to hear the Tao.'

Su Nü: 'Your Majesty's problem is a problem of all men. To make love to a woman, a man must do all proper things. He should first harmonize the atmosphere and only then can he hope his *yü hêng* will rise. The following are the details of what he must do:

    (1) He must regulate his five organs in good order.

    (2) He must know how to feel his woman's nine erotic zones.

    (3) He must know how to appreciate his woman's five beautiful qualities.

    (4) He must know how to arouse her so that he can benefit from her flooding secretions.

    (5) He should drink her saliva then his *ching* [semen] and her *chi* [breath] will be in harmony.

    (6) He should avoid the seven damages.

    (7) He should carry out the eight beneficial actions.

If he does all of these things his five organs will be regulated and his health protected and no disease will stay with him. His body will thus function smoothly. His *yü hêng* will then rise strongly each time he enters his woman.[1] Thus even his enemy will admire him and become a friend and all shame and embarrassment will become things of the past.'

1. *Unreasonable fear of impotence*

Very practical advice from Su Nü. Even with the benefit of modern science, doctors, psychologists and psychiatrists today could not give better advice to their patients. It is a straightforward encouragement. Basically she is saying

---

[1]   See 'soft entry method' described on pp.81–3.

relax, enjoy yourself and do not worry about your own erection, concentrate instead on your partner's erotic stimulation. The final sentence of the dialogue is significant. Even in ancient China, potency was a desirable quality, akin to virility. If a man could not have an erection he was ashamed and embarrassed as he would be today. All scientific evidence to the contrary, most men refuse to believe that temporary impotence is a natural and widespread occurrence. Or they believe it, but they are *still* embarrassed. But such temporary impotence is a little like catching a cold — unpleasant and irritating, but nothing to worry about. And it can easily be prevented if you have learned how. Had we treated impotence as matter-of-factly as we treat a cold, there would probably be much less of it. Unfortunately the simple remedy is easier said than done. A single incident of temporary impotence can trigger off a deep-seated fear of permanent impotence in a man. According to modern sex researchers, fear of impotence is the main factor in most cases of so-called impotence. Masters and Johnson have this to say in their book, *Human Sexual Inadequacy*:

With each opportunity for sexual connection the immediate and overpowering concern is whether or not he will be able to achieve an erection. Will he be capable of 'performing' as a 'normal man'? He is constantly concerned not only with the achieving but also with maintaining an erection of quality sufficient for intromission ... To over-simplify, it is his concern which discourages the natural occurrence of erection ... Many men contending with fears for sexual function have distorted this basic natural response to such an extent that they literally break out in cold sweat as they approach sexual opportunity.[2]

Anyone who has experienced sudden fear will always remember how dry his mouth was and how his body was drenched in cold sweat. It is truly unfortunate, or even tragic, that some men react to an opportunity to loving ecstasy with such overwhelming terror.

One other thing about impotence frightens and frustrates a man. He thinks there is nothing he can do about it. It troubled Huang Ti and it also troubled Goethe, the great German poet. He described an experience of his when he met a handsome young woman at a country inn. He was attracted to her and apparently the girl reciprocated. They managed to go to bed together with no undue difficulty but at the crucial moment his phallus refused to erect and that caused such embarrassment that he recorded his feelings in a poem which begins:

Lips on her lips and toes touch and meet

[2] *Human Sexual Inadequacy*, Chapter 1.

> *But things are not well elsewhere,*
> *What used to play the great conquering hero*
> *Now shrank like a novice down to zero.*

He went on to say that he could not command the situation; that there was nothing he could do; he could not lift a finger to help himself. His humiliation was so acute that he continued his poem by saying:

> *I'd rather be slashed in a sword fight*
> *Than be in a fix like this.*

Well, Goethe was wrong. He could have helped himself — with his fingers! If he had known the Tao of Loving, he would not have felt so helpless when his penis stayed soft. And he could have saved himself a lot of embarrassment and made the occasion a joyful one for both himself and his partner.

2. *How to overcome impotence*

The Tao of Loving has no word for 'impotence'. The ancient Chinese never thought of it as an important problem. Even in the West impotence is an over-used and misused word, more pejorative than scientific. Technically, it means the inability to perform sexual intercourse. It also carries the overtone of helplessness. If a man's penis does not rise he is not helpless. The Tao has some definite advice about dealing with this problem. He can do as Su Nü suggested: he can forget about his own erection and concentrate on his partner's body, beauty and charm. At the same time he can make sure he is giving her as much pleasure as he can without using his penis.

There are many ways of giving and receiving sexual pleasure. You can enjoy your partner's body with your hands and your lips and your tongue. Not only her looks but her smell and the feel of her skin has its own sensuous pleasure. Caressing her body's sensitive areas will arouse her. Feeling the length of her back down the spinal column, sucking her nipples gently until they harden, and beyond, kissing her vulva and tickling her clitoris with your tongue, then penetrating even deeper inside until she is inundated with her own fluid between her thighs. Her arousal, in turn, will arouse you. Her excitement can give you an erection. If it does, then your problem is solved and you can enter her vagina easily. If it does not, you can still enter her using what the Tao of Loving calls the 'soft entry' method.

3. *Soft entry method*

What soft entry actually means is that a man can enter his partner without an erection but with a little help from his fingers. If a man is experienced enough, and adroit with his hands, he can manoeuvre even a completely flaccid phallus into a woman and at the same time give both her and himself pleasure in so doing. Soft entry can even be an exciting new experience for a woman if it is well managed. Once the phallus is inside her, there is a good chance it will stiffen if the man follows the ideas of the Tao of Loving. Of course a book such as this can only suggest guidelines. There are no rigid rules to be followed. Each individual must be imaginative and flexible enough to deal suitably with different situations. Flexibility is not only plain common sense — it is a basic principle of the Tao. Where a suggestion is inapplicable, discard it. Where a suggestion works well, continue with it. With love and sex, as with most things, there are very few hard and fast rules. With these qualifications in mind, here is how to perform a successful 'soft entry':

(1) The most convenient position for soft entry are some variations on either side-by-side facing one another, or male superior position.

(2) The couple should fondle and caress each other for as long as they both enjoy it.

(3) Entry should not be attempted until the woman is thoroughly lubricated with her own liquid. If she is unable to produce sufficient liquid after a lengthy prelude, then an artificial lubricant may be necessary. The easiest and best lubricant available to use as a substitute is vegetable oil. It is made from natural ingredients which is a good recommendation for its safety and effectiveness. In an article entitled 'Life on Human Skin', which appeared in *Scientific American*, January 1969, a physician zoologist, Mary J. Marples, wrote: 'From the ecological standpoint, however, the most interesting defense mechanism is one that results from the metabolic activities of the resident flora. It has been known for some years that unsaturated fatty acids [the principle component of most vegetable oils] are an important component of sebum collected from the skin surface, and that they inhibited growth of several bacterial and fungal cutaneous pathogens.'

Vegetable oils were used for dressing wounds and skin blemishes in ancient times by physicians in both the East and the West. But any artificial or substitute lubricant should only be used as a last resort; there is nothing quite so good as the woman's natural lubricant.

(4) If the woman does not like the lubricant being applied to her, you can apply it to yourself. Rub it on the tip and shaft of your penis and it will have the same effect.

(5) The key to making the soft entry system work is the dexterity of your fingers which must be able to manoeuvre your penis into your partner's vagina. Once this is achieved your fingers will have to form a ring at the base of your phallus to make its upper part at least semi-rigid so that you can start to thrust. This finger pressure works in much the same way that pressure from a rubber band at the root of the penis would work. The finger pressure is, however, better than any artificial ring. First, you can adjust the tightness. Second, you can take your fingers away as soon as they are no longer needed and you can, in turn, reapply them whenever your phallus needs support

without having to withdraw in order to replace an artificial ring. Third, there is none of the risk to either partner of injury that artificial rings may cause.

Having reached this point most men will be able to produce an erection.

4. *Security*

The 'soft entry' technique is useful for both the skilled and the unskilled. For the novice it reduces the risk of embarrassment, and for the experienced it cuts down the failure rate. Once thrusting begins, most men can maintain an erection unless they have a serious psychological problem. 'Soft entry' shatters two stubborn myths about sex. The first is that a man cannot enter a woman unless he has achieved an erection. The second is that the erection must be sufficiently strong for intromission.

Some people might conclude that soft entry is a useful technique for men with problems, but that no normal man would need it. This is not true at all. Soft entry is not just for the beginner or the problem case. It is an integral part of the Tao of Loving. As a man becomes more practised in the Tao it becomes more important. The reason is simple. No one can be sure of an erection all the time. The soft entry method allows him to continue to enter his partner whenever she is ready for more loving.

There is no guarantee that the soft entry method will work for everyone. No system is foolproof. No system will work miracles. What soft entry can do is offer the man who learns to use it properly a very good chance of success. By 'properly' we mean depending on your physical condition at the time. Soft entry will not work if a man is physically, mentally or emotionally exhausted — or if he is undernourished or debilitated. Under normal conditions, though, it can produce the near miracle of a vagina-penis contact without a full erection to begin with.

5. *Size and shape of the phallus (and development exercises)*

From time immemorial, man has worried about the size and shape of his phallus and has had to be reassured that it is not the size but a man's sensitivity and skill with his sex organ that is important to women. In general the ancient Chinese attitude on penis size and shape agrees with the results of modern research.

For the most part, Tao of Loving texts agree that penis size and shape have little to do with the satisfaction of the female. In a dialogue with Emperor Huang Ti, his advisor Su Nü goes to great lengths to dispel his concern about the differences in men's phalli:

Huang Ti: 'Why have men's precious phalli so many variations in size and shape?'

Su Nü: 'Their phallic variations in size and shape are very much like their faces. Whether they are large or small, long or stout, hard or soft, they have already been so endowed when they were born. Sometimes a short man may have an impressively large instrument while an impressively tall man may have a short one. Some are straight and some are crooked, some have a fierce appearance. But all these characteristics do not make much difference when the phallus is in communion with the woman.'

Emperor Huang Ti: 'You mean all these differences in sizes and shapes do not at all influence the pleasure of communion?'

Su Nü: 'Difference of size and shape are only outward appearance. The true beauty and pleasure of communion are inner feelings. If a man first associates the communion with love'and respect and then treats it with true feeling what could a little difference in size and shape do to influence it adversely?'

Emperor Huang Ti: 'What about the difference in hardness and softness?'

Su Nü: 'Short and small but hard, is preferable to long and big but soft. It is however, much better to be soft and weak but gentle and sympathetic than to be hard and firm but rough and violent. The best, however, is in the middle. That is to say that the instrument is not too extreme in all respects.'

Emperor Huang Ti: 'There are some physicians who could with their skill and medicine make short and small instruments bigger and longer, weak and soft ones, harder and stronger. Could these treatments cause bad side effects? What do you think of their value?'

Su Nü: 'If the man and woman are sympathetic to each other their harmony itself could often make short and small instruments become longer and bigger and soft and weak ones become harder and stronger. When a man truly understands the Tao his instrument will not be weakened even after he had one hundred women. When a man has learned the Tao, he knows how to assist his Yang with his partner's Yin. He knows how to breathe correctly to strengthen his essence. He knows how to borrow water to help his fire. He knows how to guard his treasure, the ching, and not emit in a whole night. By so doing not only his small deficiency can be easily helped, he can even live a long life. But if a man uses medicine made from five minerals and swallows concoctions that supposedly would heighten his fire of passion, all this will only hasten the burning out of his fire and soon Yang essence will be exhausted. These artificial methods could cause great damage.'

6. *Modern attitudes*

This is somewhat like the advice a wise modern doctor would probably give patients who come to him with the same kind of complaint. Sex magazines are full of fake advertisements claiming that penis size can be increased overnight and sexual performance and desire enhanced by all sorts of magic ingredients. Most of these claims are at best ineffectual and at worst do positive harm. The plain truth is men still attach far too much importance to the size of their penis. Every serious sex manual is forced to repeat this

simple fact over and over again, and it never seems to do much good. Masters and Johnson, in their research, actually found that, in erection, a longer limp penis increases proportionately less than a small limp penis. In other words, if a penis is four inches in repose, it may grow to six inches when excited. A penis which is six inches when limp may only increase to seven inches when erect. What this means is that it does not matter what size your penis is in the shower, it is going to be adequate in the vagina. This is a difficult concept for the man with a small penis to accept. Centuries of conditioning in school locker rooms has to be overcome before such simple logic is not only universally accepted but *felt* by the man with a small penis.

7. *Wu Hsien's method*

As far as anxiety about penis size is concerned, things were much the same in ancient China. And there were some medical men who did attach some importance to penis size, in an effort to help their patients' psychological problems, just as Western doctors are forced to do today. Wu Hsien thought that penis size did make a difference to some women in achieving complete satisfaction. He, therefore, developed a method for increasing the size of what he considered a small phallus. Although it may seem unconventional, Wu Hsien's method of strengthening a man's penis certainly cannot do any harm. It consists mainly of exercise and uses no artificial preparations:

If, in communion, a man's jade stem is long and large enough to fit his partner's vulva completely, he usually can please her with less effort. It is often said that if one wishes to do a good job he must first sharpen his tool. One should know that there is a way to enlarge a deficient phallus. Every morning, any time after the hour of tzu [midnight] to before the hour of wu [noon], the time when the power of Yin is diminishing and that of Yang dominating, he should sit in a quiet room facing east meditating. He should concentrate his spirit and cut off his worries. His stomach should neither be too full nor too empty. He should expire impure air from his lungs and inhale to fill them with fresh air deep down to his abdomen. He should thus breathe deep forty-nine times. Then he should rub his palms together until they are hot as fire. Next he uses his right hand holding his scrotum and his *yü hêng*, his left hand rubs his abdomen beneath the navel in the round and round manner turning left for eighty-one times and then he uses his right hand rubbing the same spot in the same manner except turning right for another eighty-one times. Then he stretches his right hand and lifts his *yü hêng* from its root swinging and shaking it left and right hitting both legs numerous times. Then he hugs his woman and gently thrusts his *yü hêng* into her house of Yin [vulva], nurtures it with his woman's secretions and breathes in his woman's breath [in the ancient view woman's breath could be nourishing to the male and vice versa].

86

After this he should use his palms rubbing his jade peak in the manner of making a thread from fibres uncountable times. If he does this long enough he will in time notice it growing bigger and longer. [Wu does not say for how long each day nor how many days to continue this exercise. Presumably until the man has noticed that there is some effect.]

Much of this may sound just like mere ritual today, but to Taoists there is some sense in Wu Hsien's advice. They believe that every part of the human body can be trained and developed. It was based on this theory that the Chinese first developed physiotherapy. Wu's advice conforms with the Taoist belief that you must concentrate both your physical and mental efforts on a goal, and that these efforts should conform to the natural flow of Yin and Yang forces. For instance, he stipulates that the exercises should begin at a time when the Yin force is waning and the Yang force is in the ascendency. You should also be facing East when meditating. The East is where the sun (a Yang force) rises. All the man's energies are then concentrated within the Yang flow of force. Whether or not Wu's method worked I do not know because I have never tried it myself. But he had a lot of original ideas about health and his theories are usually sound; certainly it cannot hurt to try it.

It is interesting to note that in his book *Advice to Men*, the well-known author Robert Chartham has a chapter on penis size. In it, he describes his experiences with various methods of enlarging the phallus. At least two of the experiments he performed bear some relation to the ancient Chinese method in that they involve rubbing and exercising. Chartham is quick to add, 'I am right when I say that for therapeutical purposes, in so far as medical skills go, it is not possible to increase the size of the penis except in a very, very few cases. And even then, only when the penis structure is such to allow it.'

Chapter Nine

Longevity and
The Tao of Loving

P'êng Tsu said: 'A man can obtain longevity by sparing his ejaculation, by cultivating his spirit and by taking wholesome food and drink. But if he does not know the Tao of Loving, no matter what he eats or drinks, he will not live to a great age. The union of man and woman should be like the harmony of Heaven and Earth. It is because of this harmony of Yin and Yang that Heaven and Earth last forever. Man, however, has long neglected this harmony of Yin and Yang and thus is in decline of health and power. But if he could relearn the Tao of Loving to avoid ills, he will once again discover the way to longevity.'

LONGEVITY IS A CHINESE OBSESSION. WHEN MEN AND WOMEN GREW OLDER in ancient China they were treated with increased respect and honour. If they could manage to stay in good health, old age could be the best time of their lives. According to Taoist physicians, people who lived long were in harmony with the life forces of Yin and Yang, and that much nearer to the ultimate unity which perpetuated everything in Heaven and Earth. Longevity therefore was not simply a feat of time but an example to all of how life should be lived. The respect accorded the elderly was in recognition of this.

1. *Love-making and longevity*
In ancient China the correct way of love-making was linked to good health. Without exception, all the ancient texts stress that practising the Tao of Loving is the single most important factor in lengthening life. In terms which seem unscientific to us, the ancient Chinese managed to arrive at some very up-to-date conclusions.

A dialogue between Emperor Huang Ti and Su Nü deals with medical effects of practising the Tao. The emperor was at this time tired of making love and he told Su Nü:

Emperor Huang Ti: 'I do not think I want to make love any more. What do you think of that?'
Su Nü: 'No, you must not do that. Heaven and Earth have their opening and closing,

Yin and Yang have their activities and changes. We human beings must not do things against nature. Now Your Majesty wants to refrain from love-making and that is against nature. When Yin and Yang are not in communion they can no longer compensate and harmonize each other. We breathe so that we can exchange old and used air for fresh air. When the jade stem is not active it will atrophy. That is why it must be regularly exercised. If one can make love and yet knows how to control and regulate one's emissions one can benefit greatly from this. And that is what we call the return of the ching. The return of ching is beneficial to man's health.'

On another occasion the Emperor asked Su Nü: 'In Yin and Yang communion a correct proportion is vital. I should like to hear about it.'

Su Nü: 'When a couple practise the Tao of Loving correctly the male will remain healthy and youthful and the female will avoid a hundred diseases. Both will enjoy it thoroughly and at the same time increase their physical strength. But if they do not know how to practise it correctly then love-making can be harmful to their health. In order to receive full benefit from the Tao the couple must first learn how to breathe long and deeply so that they will be relaxed. They must have a sense of security so that their hearts will be tranquil. They must achieve an accord of their wills so that there will be no conflict. When they have succeeded in all three essentials the Tao will be completely at their service. They must also pay attention to practical matters such as temperature so that it is neither too cold nor too warm, to their stomachs so that they are neither too full nor too empty. Also they must take the act easy so that they thrust neither too fast nor too deeply. A good guideline is when the female is completely satisfied and the male is not yet exhausted.'

2. *Modern cult of youth*

Longevity is no longer only a Chinese obsession. Nowadays people do not always use the term 'longevity', but that is what they mean. In the West, we make a cult of youth. In both America and Europe, the last ten years have seen a passion to stay youthful among older people. Men and women who, ten years ago, would have retired gracefully to their gardening and their knitting are now taking up 'young' sports like skiing and skin-diving. Their clothes, their hair, their complexion, their demeanour all reflect a desire to keep hold of the joys and vigour of youth. Even their ideas are often adapted to keep up with the young. And why not? For those who practise the Tao all this is quite easy to achieve. Equally, students of the Tao understand deeply the words of Pao Pu Tzu (Ko Hung), the well-known Tao master of the fourth century: 'Best medicine and nourishment of the whole world cannot help you if you do not know and believe the Tao of Loving...'

90

Despite the ornate language, the ancient Chinese wisdom in love and sex has a sound basis in natural science. For one thing, our sex organs are like all our other organs — they need regular use and exercise in order to stay strong and healthy. In addition, modern science has established that hormones are closely linked with the ageing process, and our sexual machinery includes vital hormone-producing glands. On a psychological level too, love-making gives a boost to the human spirit. Nobody likes to feel too old for love. Those who can continue to feel, whatever their age, that they can love and be loved are a long way towards escaping the terrible sense of loneliness and isolation so many older people suffer.

Some people believe that the sex drive disappears after middle-age. This is another myth. It may be true that the urge to make love diminishes in some individuals, but by no means in all. Masters and Johnson found a correlation between the age at which you begin sexual activity and the age at which you stop. The sooner you begin, it seems, the longer you go on. Also, the more active you are sexually when young, the more likely you are to continue being active into old age. There is no reason at all why men and women cannot continue to make love right through their lives.

3. *Ejaculation in middle life*

What does diminish is the male urge to ejaculate in later life. Since Western men do not usually understand that ejaculation and orgasm are not the same thing, they think they have begun to fail. Simone de Beauvoir, in her book *Old Age*, gives a graphic description of how this misconception affected a man called Paul Léautaud. De Beauvoir writes: 'We have one most remarkable piece of evidence concerning an old man's relationship with his body, his image and his sex; this is Léautaud's journal . . .'[1] According to de Beauvoir, Léautaud meets a woman very much to his liking when he is fifty and she is fifty-five. He calls her 'Madame' and describes her as 'a truly passionate woman, wonderfully equipped for pleasure and exactly to my taste in these matters.' Seven years later a great deal of this compatibility has disappeared. He could not make love so often now and the love affair reaches a second stage: 'We are attached to each other only through our senses — by vice — and what remains is utterly tenuous.' He no longer calls her 'Madame' but 'the Panther' instead. This is similar to what ineffectual and insecure men in ancient China called their women. Men who were hard-pressed to perform sexually by unsatisfied

[1]   *Old Age*, p.340.

partners would recite an old proverb: Women in their thirties are like wolves. Women in their forties are like tigers.

In both instances the name-calling simply reflects the worn-out state of the man rather than the sexual appetite of the woman. What Léautaud did was normal for men of his time and today — he cut down on love-making at the expense of his own happiness and well-being, and his mistress's. Two years later when he was fifty-nine the third stage of the affair began. He started calling her 'the Scourge'. He was still attracted to her but was fearful that too much loving might be fatal to him. His journals take a gloomy turn: 'What a feeble ejaculation when I make love: little better than water!' Making love tired him and his doctor advised him to give it up. He tried to, but not completely; he also started masturbating. Those who know the Tao will understand immediately that this was no solution. Masturbation for the man is the loss of male essence with no compensating gain of female essence. There is no harmony of Yin and Yang and the act is futile. It was for Léautaud. He suffered from wanting to make love but not daring to. He missed the pleasure of seeing and fondling a naked woman. His old age was spent in 'deep sorrow'. The picture is all too familiar. Léautaud was no more foolish than most of us would be in the same situation. Masters and Johnson's research bears out what the ancient Chinese knew so many centuries ago. They state in no uncertain terms that an older man can be an effective lover *provided* he does not force himself to ejaculate.

4. *Ejaculation control and longevity*

There are many stories about longevity in the Tao of Loving manuscripts. It is fairly safe to say an element of exaggeration may have entered some of these tales. While the ancient Chinese — and even the present-day Chinese — are noted for their hardiness, to talk of men who lived to two hundred, or even one hundred and fifty years smacks of exaggeration. But what is not so far-fetched is the reason for their long lives — and even allowing for exaggeration they are still long lives! How did the masters manage to stay healthy and vigorous well into their eighties, nineties and hundreds; years in which most people would expect to be feeble, sick or even bedridden? In a dialogue, Su Nü explains it to Huang Ti:

Huang Ti: 'I have heard that men of the great antiquity lived over two hundred years. And men of the middle antiquity lived up to one hundred and twenty years. But men of our time often die before they reach the age of thirty. So few men are relaxed and at peace with themselves these days and so many of them are suffering from diseases. What do you think is the reason for this?'

Su Nü: '. . . [the reason] men often die young today is that they do not know the secret of the Tao. They are young and passionate and they emit their ching indiscriminately when they love. It is like cutting off the roots and the fountain of their lives . . . How can they expect to live long?'

5. *A brief history of longevity in China*

According to tradition Huang Ti himself — a devoted follower of the Tao of Loving — lived to be 111 years old. Five of his next six successors lived to be 98, 105, 117, 99 and 100 years old respectively. These figures are from Ssuma Ch'ien's *Shih Chi* ('Historical Records'). Later historians by and large have accepted these figures as valid. Let us accept them also and examine the possible reasons for such longevity. One reason might be pure coincidence, or inherited genetic traits. Another — which does not preclude the second — is that Huang Ti practised the Tao of Loving and passed it on to his children and they in turn to their children.

Delving further into history, we find that over the entire three thousand years of recorded history in China, no other emperors lived as long as Huang Ti and his descendants. In fact many of them did not live long — by any standards. The Tao of Loving could provide a possible explanation. After the death of the sixth of Huang Ti's successors, the Tao of Loving was gradually forgotten. It was not until the sixth century B.C. that the Tao was revived by Lao Tzu, the author of the *Tao Tê Ching*. Only the sketchiest information about this remarkable old man survives. According to the *Historical Records*, his family name was Li. *Lao* in Chinese means 'old' and Lao Tzu is reputed to have lived between 160 and 200 years. Ssuma Ch'ien comments in his *Historical Records*: 'He lived so long because he was cultivating the Tao.'

Scattered over the next 2,500 years of Chinese history are individual instances of longevity. In nearly every case, they practised the Tao of Loving. Interest in the Tao revived again during the Early Han Dynasty (206 B.C.–A.D. 24). In the official Dynastic History, there is a list of the most important books in circulation at the time. Eight are books on the Tao of Loving. The most important was a book by Jung Chêng Kung. But it was not until the second part of the Han Dynasty, known as Later Han, that we find actual evidence of longevity due to the practising of the Tao of Loving. The official history of that period, the *Hou Han Shu*, contains a biography of the Taoist physician and surgeon Hua T'o, who lived to be about a hundred and remained youthful and professionally active until his death. Nor did he die of old age. He was executed by Ts'ao Ts'ao, a ruthless politician who was angry because Hua T'o refused to remain as his personal physician. If his life had not been ended in this way, who knows how long Hua T'o might have lived? His biographer comments that the Han Dynasty was especially rich in men of unusual talents and achievements. Special mention is made of three men – Lêng Shou Kuang, T'ang Yu and Lu Nü Sheng – all of them instructed by Jung Cheng Kung and practitioners of the Tao of Loving. Lêng Shou Kuang lived to be over 150 and is said to have looked like a man of 30 or 40.

Another interesting example during the Han Dynasty involves Wu Tzu Tu, a son-in-law of the Imperial House. One day when the Emperor Shou Wo was out hunting on the banks of the Wei River, he noticed that Wu Tzu Tu, who was 138 years old at the time, had an unusual aura about him. The Emperor asked his attendant, Tungfang Shuo, about the old man. He replied: 'This man's life force is in communication with heaven because he practises the Tao of Loving.' The Emperor ordered his attendants to leave so he could talk to Wu Tzu Tu alone. He asked about the Tao of Loving and Wu told him:

The Tao of Loving is a difficult secret: that is why I, Your Majesty's servant, have never said anything about it before. Also because few people can really practise it and that is one more reason I did not dare to reveal it before. I was taught the Tao by Ling Yang Tzu [one of the Tao Masters] when I was a very sick man of sixty-five years of age and till now I have practised the Tao for seventy-three years. All those who strive for longevity must seek at the source of life. And the secret of this is not forcing ejaculation even when one is greatly attracted by the beauty of one's female partner. Forcing ejaculation will cause all kinds of disease.

According to Ko Hung (Pao Pu Tzu), Wu Tzu Tu was about 200 years old when he died. If he did not start practising the Tao until he was 65 he must have had long personal experience of forced ejaculation. It is interesting that he stressed this point to the Emperor.

It was not until nearly a thousand years later that another interesting case of longevity is fully recorded.[2] The reason may be that fewer and fewer people knew the Tao of Loving in these later periods. However, during the Ming Dynasty (A.D. 1368–1643) we find a man who calls himself 'the greybeard of ninety-five years from Chekiang province'. He wrote as follows in a reprint of two Tao of Loving books:

[2] Except for the case of Sun S'sû-Mo, see 'Summing Up'.

94

During the reign of Emperor Shih Tsung [A.D. 1522–1566][3] at the Imperial Court in Peking, a Taoist, Tou Chen-jen enjoyed the Imperial favour because of his magic skills. But his knowledge of the Tao of Loving was very real. The fact that the Emperor reached such an advanced age was entirely due to the Tao of Loving taught to him by the Taoist. Being interested in the Tao, I bribed a palace official and thus obtained copies of the Taoist's two secret books, *Chi Chi Chen Ching* and *Hsiu Chen Yen Yi* written by Lu Tung-Pin of the T'ang Dynasty [A.D. 618–906] and Hu Hsien of the Han Dynasty, respectively. When I tried to put what I read from these two books into practice I found it difficult at first, but after some time it became a natural habit. In the course of sixty years I have loved more than one hundred women, reared seventeen sons,[4] and served under five emperors. Though now I am advanced in years I am not yet tired of loving and could still satisfy several women in one night. Though Heaven has blessed me with a long life I cannot deny that the Tao of Loving has a great deal to do with it. As the ancient proverb says: Those who monopolize their skill and knowledge will come to no good end. Also a man's life-span does not last much beyond a hundred years and I could not bear the thought that these two books will become lost when I come to die some day. Thus I had them reprinted wishing that all men in this world may benefit from them and reach the advanced age of P'êng Tsu. If there are skeptics who doubt the validity of these books let them cast away their chances of attaining longevity. Why should I worry about them? Written in the first lunar month of the Spring of the year 1594 by the greybeard of ninety-five years from Chekiang at the Purple Mushroom Hall of the Tien Tai Mountain.

[3] The reign is better known as the Chia-Ch'ing period. Due mainly I think to his anti-Buddhist policy, the reputation he left behind is not a very good one. But for myself I rather like the development of art during his reign. Particularly beautiful are the multi-coloured, decorated porcelain wares and cloisenné. The reign was the second longest of the dynasty, exceeded by only two years by the Wan-Li Emperor.

[4] A prejudice against women in those days caused him to omit the number of daughters he had.

Chapter Ten

May – September Relationships

There is a quarrelsome couple on the East side of the street with a husband who is young and impressively handsome.
There is a loving, harmonious couple on the West side of the street with a husband who is old and nothing to look at.
Why?
It is simply that the unimpressive looking old man knows how to satisfy his woman and the good-looking young one does not.

AN ANONYMOUS TAO OF LOVING MASTER WROTE THIS DIALOGUE TO illustrate a point about loving and age. In a society that practised the Tao, where longevity increased and where ageing was not accompanied by infirmity, the usual rules did not apply. People of very different ages could marry and live together happily.

To begin with, a person's age did not mean the same as it does now. A man who is over 65 today is thought to be entering his declining years. But for those who practised the Tao, 65 was not an exceptionally old age. They could look forward to 30 or 40 more years of vigorous good health. Men and women who were 65 could easily love partners who were 20 or 30. What would nowadays be called a 'May–December' romance was more like a 'May–September' romance for the followers of the Tao.

Most of the ancient Tao of Loving texts specifically recommend this sort of relationship. One book, the *Su Nü Ching*, has this to say:

If an old man is mated with an equally old woman even when they do have a child it will not as a rule live to a ripe old age.

But when a man of eighty years is mated with a girl of eighteen years or even fifteen years they can have children who as a rule will live long lives. And if a woman of fifty years can have a young man, she can often still have a child.

1. *Society's prejudice*
In the West, the 'sexual revolution' of the past few years has made 'May–September' romances more open and more acceptable than they once were.

However, society is still prejudiced against them. People still tend to 'talk' and to view such couples as if they were engaged in some sort of perversion. Charlie Chaplin and Oona O'Neill are one famous couple who raised eyebrows and drew smiles when they married. She was only seventeen and he was then fifty-four and thrice divorced, but they were strong enough not to suffer from the worst effects of social prejudice. They went on to confound their detractors by having a very happy and successful marriage.

2. *Young woman—older man relationships*

Those who know the Tao of Loving are not surprised by a success story like this. They know that a relationship between an older man and a young woman has some real advantages. First, an older man is often slow to erect in response to foreplay. For him, a young woman who produces ample vaginal lubrication quickly is a blessing. He can insert his phallus into her vagina without a full erection more easily. After entering such a lush environment, it is a simple matter for a man who knows the Tao to become fully erect. And on her part she may find such gentle, slower procedure enchanting and preferable to a young man's frighteningly sudden erection, abrupt insertion and swift ejaculation.

Secondly, a younger woman not only produces ample lubrication fast but she also sustains lubrication far longer. In most cases this fountain is very nearly inexhaustible as long as she is stimulated in some way. And this benefits them both. Just as he is slow to erect, he is even slower to finish, an essential factor which could bring her to an ecstatic bliss and which many inexperienced young men are not able to do. An older man and a young woman could make a superb combination. Third, young women exude a natural smell of youth and freshness that easily excites an older man. To complement this, he will contribute an atmosphere of calm and confidence which very few inexperienced young men could command. And fourth and most important, a young woman has a much tighter vagina which grips and excites the older and more experienced lover. If a man practises the Tao he will know how to control his ejaculation even under such exciting circumstances. This will also give the young woman a great pleasure because she could sense his joy of excitement and profound appreciation, while a young man may regard it as a great hazard or even a trap.

3. *Older man—older woman relationships*

These advantages do not always apply in a relationship between an older man and a woman of the same age. Sometimes older women find it hard to keep going through vigorous and sustained love-making. Sometimes their vaginas cannot supply sufficient lubrication, usually one or two short love-making periods in an evening is all they can manage. It often takes a lot of work on a man's part to get even that much lubrication. He must stimulate her much more intensely and for a much longer time than a younger woman. Artificial lubricant may help but it is an inferior substitute, and this may explain why sometimes vigorous elderly men lose interest in their equally elderly mates, or develop a real or imagined impotency. But if they have the chance to make love to an attractive young woman their recovery will be swift.

4. *The attraction is not always one-sided*

The attraction between older men and young women is by no means always one-sided. Many young women prefer older men as partners in love. However, they do so in the face of considerable social prejudice. While many older men can provide a sense of security for a young woman, their attraction (contrary to popular belief) most frequently is not at all based on material opulence. These are men who have had ample experience in both the joys and sorrow of loving and have thus learned through the years the true meaning of tenderness. And many girls do find such men attractive mainly for this reason.

Another factor is the fear some young women have of getting old themselves. If a young woman marries a contemporary, she worries that one day he may decide to leave her for a younger woman. For women like this there is a certain feeling of safety in marrying an older man. Knowing that he will be seventy when she is forty-five does not seem so dangerous. (The preceeding sentence is almost exactly what Edna O'Brien told Nell Dunn in the latter's book entitled *Talking to Women*.)

All these are sound reasons for an older man—younger woman relationship; but it is going to be quite some time before such relationships are accepted for what they are. How many mothers would want or even allow their daughters to have a very much older man? How many older women are there who are open-minded enough without harbouring feelings of resentment against a young woman who marries in that way?

5. *Advantages of older woman—young man relationships*

One thing that might speed up a more enlightened attitude is if society was

less harsh towards older woman—young man relationships. In fact, of course, society condemns them even more cruelly. Older women are accused of everything from silliness to nymphomania. In reality there is not always anything silly or abnormal about such a relationship. On the contrary, there is a lot to be said for it on both sides.

As we have already noted in the chapter on ejaculation control, an older woman can be more sympathetic and understanding of a young man's sexual difficulties than a partner of his own age. In the case of a shy or hesitant youth, this can be very important for his sexual well-being. Another point is that an older woman, especially if she has had children, often has a less tight vagina which is particularly good for a young man who has not developed full ejaculation control. A less tight vagina is not so suitable for an older man who has mastered the Tao of Loving because it does not provide him with enough stimulation.

Young men have erections almost instantly when aroused. This can be very exciting for some experienced older women, just as a young vagina can stimulate an older man. Seeing and fondling the fully erect, hard and swollen *yü hêng* of a young man could make an older woman lubricate enough for an inspired period of love-making. An older man might not arouse her to anything like the same extent.

Young men in turn could be attracted to older women for the same reasons that young girls prefer older men. Their gentleness and their experience are key factors. Some men enjoy the attention they get when an older woman's maternal instincts are aroused. Some younger men find such a combination of sexual and maternal love irresistible.

It is tragic, therefore, that these relationships have to be carried on secretly and furtively. If we could all be somewhat more understanding we would see they are something to encourage and not to condemn. And we could be well on the way to solving the problems of many lonely older women and shy young men.

6. *Personal hygiene*

May—September relationships as a rule encourage older men and women not to let themselves go. But there are still far too many people, old or not so old, who do not fully realize the importance of their appearance or even of personal hygiene and suffer greatly from loneliness as a result. Bertrand Russell in his *Autobiography* told how bad breath nearly wrecked his relationship with an attractive young woman: 'I was suffering from pyorrhea although I did not know it, and this caused my breath to be offensive, which also I did not know. She could not bring herself to mention it, and it was only after I had discovered the trouble and had it cured that she let me know how much it had ·affected her.'

Russell's experience is not unique and it reminds us that we should take great care to get bad breath cleared up quickly both because it may indicate that something is seriously wrong and because it is offensive to others.

7. *Conclusions*
One of the consequences of the sexual revolution should be a steady increase in the number of and the acceptance of May—September relationships. People often think of the older person being the lucky one to 'catch' a young lover; but it works both ways. A young and inexperienced partner can learn a lot and enjoy a lot more while he or she is learning from an older lover. In fact many younger women or younger men truly began to relish loving ecstatically only after such an experience. Two virgins is the classic recipe for sexual disaster.

If we have any reservations about May—September relationships, it is this: it could be dangerous for an older man who does not know the Tao of Loving to get involved with a highly sexed young woman. Her attractiveness and her love demands might prove irresistible and he could overspend his sexual energy. The answer to this problem, of course, is mastering the Tao of Loving. It is almost ideally designed for people in this situation to derive the greatest benefit from the harmony of Yin and Yang while conserving their energy.

Chapter Eleven

Breathing, T'ai Chi Ch'uan and The Tao of Loving

THE ANCIENT TAO OF LOVING MASTERS CONSIDERED LOVE, FOOD AND exercise the three columns supporting a man's life. Longevity depended on the strength of these pillars. Though your health would undoubtedly improve through practising the Tao, you also had to attend to the other two pillars, food and exercise — in particular, breathing exercises.

1. *Proper breathing*

Proper breathing is a science in itself, and beyond the scope of this book. According to Taoist masters breath or *chi* is one of the vital life forces and not just in the material way that it provides oxygen and gets rid of carbon dioxide. This is merely the visible manifestation of breathing. There is another, invisible function of breathing. From it man draws in the unseen cosmic power of the Universe. Even in the modern scientific West physicians and researchers have in recent years observed that the lungs are not merely organs of gas exchange for the blood.[1]

2. *Breathing exercises*

To some people, it may seem that the Taoists stress proper breathing out of all proportion, but in truth we cannot stress it enough. We simply do not exist without it. It is essential to our spiritual as well as to our physical health. For instance, proper diaphragmatic breathing is basic to almost all forms of meditation. It is also fundamental to Taoist medical therapy. In China today, this Taoist medical practice has once again been revived and has been found particularly useful in the treatment of abdominal disorders. Deep breathing lies at the root of good health. It is a very simple and economic way to make ourselves stronger. Three essential points will help you breathe the right way:

---

[1] The subject has been reported by *Science News* (Washington D.C.), September 6th, 1975, as their news of the week entitled 'The Role of Lungs Expanding: Air Sacs to Endocrine Glands'.

(1) Keep your posture straight and your chest natural.

(2) Learn to breathe in and out with your diaphragm and your nose only. Do not use your mouth.

(3) First exhale everything in your lungs slowly and then empty them completely by making a last effort to contract your diaphragm. Now breathe in gently by expanding your diaphragm to the utmost. And then once again exhale slowly and repeat the whole process.

Naturally you will not breathe this way all the time, but you should do it for at least a few minutes daily so that deep and slow diaphragmatic breathing will become a natural habit even when you are asleep.

3. *Improving the organs*

The ancient Taoists believed that every part of the body, including the sex organs, could be strengthened and improved by correct exercise. They devised movements for nearly every part of the body. There were, for example, eye exercises to improve the sight and a whole host of others. They believed that eye exercises could not only maintain perfect vision as we grow older, but could even remedy defective eyesight in some cases. Aldous Huxley, in a book called *The Art of Seeing*, tells how he saved himself from going blind by exercise when all medical means had failed him. He never actually states that his exercises were based on Taoist theories, but the book contains many passages that are Taoist in character:

Impress upon yourself the fact that, among persons with defective sight, there is a regular correlation between attentive looking and quite unnecessary, indeed positively harmful, interference with breathing . . . Therefore fill your lungs with the stuff — not violently, as though you were doing deep breathing exercises, but in an easy effortless way, expiration following inspiration in a natural rhythm. Continue, while breathing in this way, to pay attention to the thing you want to see . . . Any improvement in the quality of circulation is reflected immediately in better vision . . . [2]

Note the connection between quality of sight, better circulation and correct breathing. Not only do eyes not function properly but our entire constitution suffers when we are not breathing correctly. C.G. Jung, the famous psychiatrist, noticed that both neurotics and tuberculosis patients breathe in a panting, superficial way which does not sufficiently ventilate the lungs.[3] Incredibly it seems that most of us do not use more than one sixth of our total lung capacity.

[2] Aldous Huxley, *The Art of Seeing*, pp.44—5.
[3] Quoted in Michel Cattier, *The Life and Work of Wilhelm Reich*, translated by Boulanger, p.196.

Love-making in itself is another important exercise for the body, but it is not enough. It does not exercise all the muscles of the body. Your own experience will tell you — if you stay in bed much over eight hours you will start to get a backache or feel uncomfortable in one way or another. A brisk walk, a bicycle ride or a couple of sets of tennis — any physical exercise — will put you right. A great number of people have trouble with their spinal columns, especially as they grow older. Even young people have rounded backs, while nearly all the complaints of the elderly revolve around a backache of some kind. And you cannot do much love-making with an aching back.

4. *T'ai Chi Ch'uan*
The ancient Chinese designed a series of exercises to relieve all these symptoms. It is called *T'ai Chi Ch'uan*. You have probably heard of it as a martial art, like judo. The Japanese Judo technique is itself based on the philosophy of the Tao, in Chinese it is actually called Ju-Tao. T'ai Chi Ch'uan is a similar defence technique using only the bare hands and fists. T'ai Chi represents the harmony of Yin and Yang and Ch'uan in Chinese means 'fist'. Properly performed, T'ai Chi Ch'uan is like a graceful dance. In fact, it originally began as a dance. Its invention is ascribed to the time of the legendary Emperor Fu-Hsi (who came well before Emperor Huang Ti and who is credited with teaching the people how to tame wild animals for domestic service) who asked Yin Kang to fashion a 'Great Dance' for his people so that they could exercise themselves joyfully and ward off diseases. Later, during the Han Dynasty, a famous physician and surgeon already mentioned, Hua T'o, contributed to the development of the art of T'ai Chi Ch'uan. Hua T'o was a keen observer of nature and wild life, and felt that animals had a lot to teach man about keeping their bodies fit and strong.

T'ai Chi Ch'uan is also called 'long Ch'uan' because all its sequences are smoothly connected without a break. It should be done in as lively and agile a way as spinning a wheel. It is also called the 'soft Ch'uan' because you are not supposed to use brute force to overcome an adversary; but by seizing the right moment and the right position you can use your adversary's strength to throw him off balance. There is a Taoist saying: 'Four ounces of strength can throw a mass of a thousand pounds.'

5. *T'ai Chi as a means of self-defence and a superb exercise*
T'ai Chi Ch'uan is a means of self-defence as well as a superb exercise. If a

105

defence technique is what you want, we would advise you to find a competent teacher, but if an excellent exercise is what you want, then after a few lessons you could easily keep on exercising every day. We say it is a superb and excellent exercise because it is not strenuous and it can be done nearly any time any place by almost anyone regardless of age, sex and physical condition. Yet it is extremely effective in keeping a person in 'total fitness'. This term is borrowed from L.E. Morehouse's popular book.[4] We like this term not only because it fits perfectly with our description, but also because Morehouse's theory of gentle exercises is rather close to that of the T'ai Chi Ch'uan which also is not a hard exercise; the secret of its effectiveness is that it softly exercises all one's joints. Combined with the deep breathing, it could easily preserve one's youth. For most people feel and show their age through their stiff or even painful joints. When this happens they cannot use their bodies properly any longer, and their health rapidly deteriorates.

6. *Diet*

The third pillar of good health in the Taoist philosophy is food. The ancient Chinese had much the same things to say about eating as Western nutritionists say today. Sun S'sû-Mo, the celebrated seventh-century Taoist physician whom we have so often mentioned, wrote: 'A truly good physician first finds out the cause of the illness, and having found out that, he tries first to cure it by food. Only when food fails does he prescribe medication.' This is not much different from what Tom Spies, the Dean of American nutritionists, had to say more recently: 'If we only knew enough, all disease could be prevented and cured through proper nutrition.'

Eating as a pleasure is relatively unimportant to a man who practises the Tao. But he is concerned about eating as a way to keep well and improve his health. Nutrition was taken very seriously in ancient China and it should be just as important for us today. There are many good modern books on the subject, so there is no reason for not knowing what to eat. Even without reading, it is easy to know what is good for you by simply observing the effect different foods have on your digestion and general health. In today's affluent society, we are all tempted to eat and drink too much. Over-eating is one of the worst things one can do to one's body. We'd all be better off spending less time at the table and more time making love.

[4] *Total Fitness.*

Chapter Twelve

Learning The Tao

Something words and voice will arouse
those who are romantic.
And touching your *yü hêng*
those that are lustful . . .

WU HSIEN

LEARNING THE TAO OF LOVING IS NOT REALLY DIFFICULT IF YOU START
with the premise that it involves the acceptance of very different concepts
from Western ones. We all have preconceived notions which are difficult to
shed. It takes strong arguments to move us from our accustomed ways. But
the Tao offers us good reasons for changing some of our ideas of loving. For
instance, many women reject the idea of 'skill' or 'technique' in love-making.
And quite rightly. In current usage it has come to mean the method of love-
making used by a 'professional' and it is insulting to women. 'Technique'
without warmth, feeling or emotion takes the heart out of making love. On
the other hand, the Chinese Taoists, while emphasizing a tender and highly
sensitive attitude towards love and sex still equally stress the importance of
skill. Their idea is that if you want to do something well, you must
develop the proper skills. If you want to play the piano, you have first to
learn finger exercises, and then practise them daily. If you want to paint,
you first have to learn composition and how to draw. In the same way, men
and women must learn how to love if they are going to be effective partners.
Balzac said, over a century ago, that an unskilled lover is like a monkey who
tries to play the violin. And he was right. An unskilled lover can make a
woman feel as if he is simply masturbating in her vagina. Germaine Greer
in *The Female Eunuch* has described this kind of experience: 'When a man
is ashamed to masturbate, and instead waylays a woman for the sake of
finding sexual release, the shame that should attach to the masturbatory
activity, not significantly different in such a case except that the friction
was provided by a female organ and the ejaculation may occur in the vagina,
is referred to the woman. The man regards her as a receptacle into which he

107

has emptied his sperm, a kind of human spittoon, and turns from her in disgust.'[1]

The Tao suggests that a man develop his loving skills so that he can both satisfy and appreciate his love partner. 'Satisfaction' in this Taoist sense is not only the attainment of immediate pleasure but in a deeper more meta-physical sense involves the cultivation of a mutual tranquillity. When the Tao of Loving talks about 'technique', it does not just mean your ability to thrust and ejaculate in a controlled way, but the development of all your senses so that you can arrive at a true harmony of Yin and Yang. Love-making then is not just a mechanical thing but a total experience. A pianist can develop a mastery of fingering technique but he is still nothing more than a technician. It is only when he brings his full senses and imagination to bear on his music that he becomes a true artist. Loving ecstatically is very much like that.

1. *Sensory development*

To some extent we are all victims of our puritanical past and our artificial present. We must learn to reactivate our sense of smell, for example, perhaps the sense in loving second in importance only to touching. We are constant-ly bombarded by advertisements for deodorants for just about every part of our body until we are so over-douched and over-soaped that we almost smell like perfumed plastics just out of the factory. We have lost sight of the fact that, in nature, men and women are instinctively attracted to each other by their individual special natural scent. Often they are more aroused by the way a member of the opposite sex smells than by anything else. A person's particular fragrance of skin, hair, mouth, genitals etc. can be most pleasing or even overwhelmingly exciting to an especially congenial person. And this may at least partly explain the popular yet mysterious term 'chemical attraction'. Of course there may be others who are repelled by the strong, pungent natural odour of the vagina. Still, to get rid of the smell by excessive spraying or douching may upset the natural balance of secretions and organisms in the vaginal environment and cause infection. We are not against cleanliness or simple hygiene. Just the opposite. What we are saying is that, for most people, men and women, simple hygiene and scrupulous cleanliness is all that is needed.

Equally in need of development is the sense of touch. In Victorian times, people made love with their clothes on. There was no direct body contact

[1] *The Female Eunuch*, p.253.

except for the genitals. Well, fewer wear clothes in bed these days, but we still tend to confine sex to genital contact. There is all the difference in the world between mechanical genital sex and loving with the whole body and all the senses open. Body touching for both men and women is essential to the truly satisfying love experience. Loving should be a harmonious co-operation between men and women in which your hands and every other part of your body gives and receives pleasure. Here is how:

(1) While making love, neither of you should stop touching each other with your hands, until you are both tired and ready to go to sleep.

(2) A woman's clitoris and breasts are usually her m sensitive spots. But do not touch her here immediately: caress her hands and kiss her first. A woman is also sensitive on or near the spinal column from the head to the hips and thighs. These points vary from woman to woman but the most popular ones are the ears, the back of the neck and around the waist, especially in the back. The inside of the thigh is also very sensitive. Her abdomen is often effectively caressed by your abdomen — one of the great joys of loving.

(3) For men, the most sensitive areas apart from the phallus are the inside of the ear and, in some men, the chest. About 50 per cent of men have nipple erections. Also try the inside of the thigh.

(4) One of the secrets of successful body touching is to make contact from head to toe at as many points as you can. Touching in loving should not be static. Keep your hands flowing over your partner's body; your own body responding to the subtle variations as she breathes or moves against you.

(5) At the start of love-making, women should concentrate on complete body touching rather than on stimulating the phallus by hand. The exception would be for those women who are quickly aroused by touching a swelling *yü hêng*. Also, if prolonged body contact does not induce an erection in the man, the woman should of course use her hands on his penis. Older men react differently from younger men when you touch their genitals. A young man's phallus is usually more sensitive and quicker to ejaculate. It should be touched lightly along its whole length. Apply a slight pressure near the root and almost none on the glans penis. An older man's penis can be handled much more firmly. He does not erect or ejaculate so fast. The best way to produce an erection in an older man is to use both hands on him. You can easily stimulate a penis with cupped hands: most men find this very exciting for it reminds them of entering the vagina. Be careful you do not apply too much pressure to the foreskin if your partner is not circumcised. This can sometimes cause irritation. Instead, you should concentrate the caress on the glans penis and the testicles. Inexperienced women tend to ignore the testicles and the scrotum. Experienced women fully understand their importance. Older men love to have their testicles felt. Handle with care though! The best way is to cup the entire scrotum with your hand while you stimulate the end of it and the root of the phallus with your finger-tips. Do not squeeze too hard whatever you do.

In a younger man this kind of stimulation might make him come very quickly, so be careful. Use your hand gently for the best results and be prepared for very different reactions from different men. Some may be so aroused they come in your hand while others will not even erect entirely.

(6) Men should take care of their hands so they are smooth and clean. Very few women enjoy rough handling. Most women feel like Marlene Dietrich who said, 'All real men are gentle; without tenderness, a man is uninteresting.' Remember that your hands are going to be in some very delicate places. Many women are used to having their clitoris stimulated by fingers and can neither be fully aroused nor reach orgasm without extensive but delicate help from your fingers or their own. A rough or dirty finger can cause them irritation or even infection. Then there are some women who need their nipples fondled before they can reach a climax. On the other hand, you may find a woman who dislikes digital stimulation of any kind – you will have to find this out by trial and error. It may be that total body contact is what turns her on, but she detests your fingers on her vulva. A woman like this can be extremely interesting to many men who are not overly fond of digital manipulation.

2. *Learning to communicate*

Besides learning to touch each other, we need to learn to communicate with each other as well. It is not simply what you say but how you say it. In a way, we are all still like babies. We react to sounds rather than actual words. This is particularly true in love-making.

Freud has shown us that sexual behaviour is deeply rooted in infancy when we are conditioned by our mother's tender touch and soothing voice. The entertainment industry has always known the value of a sexy voice. The human voice is a mysterious and wonderful instrument. Yours should be too. Silence during love-making can unnerve your partner. It can be interpreted as lack of interest or dissatisfaction. We are not suggesting you have a philosophical dialogue – just that you show signs of approval and satisfaction. Here are some important points:

(1) Complete silence may be construed as dissatisfaction.
(2) Avoid using harsh or negative words or sounds. A successful love session requires a harmonious and appreciative atmosphere.
(3) Never criticize. It can have a devastating effect on love-making. No matter how virile your partner, he will lose self-confidence if you attack him at his most vulnerable moment – when he is making love.
(4) Praise with sweet soft voice can often perform magic.

3. *The Tao is not only for men*

In a slightly lesser degree women also need to understand the Tao. For example, unless the female partner knows the Tao she may be hurt or offended when her man does not ejaculate. She may think she has not pleased him. That she has failed to satisfy him. She too will have to learn

that orgasm and ejaculation are not one and the same thing. This is fundamental to the Tao of Loving, but it is a principle which has also been
recognized by Kinsey: 'But orgasm may occur without the emission of
semen ... It also occurs among a few male adults ... who deliberately
constrict their genital muscles (five cases) in the contraceptive technique
which is known as coitus reservatus. These males experience real orgasm
which they have no difficulty in recognizing, even if it is without ejaculation.'[2] This problem may be further complicated because some women feel
that a part of their satisfaction comes from feeling the man ejaculate inside
them. This is a small point set against the benefits of the Tao of Loving.
What woman would not rather have a man who can make love all night —
and still ejaculate at the end of the session — than a man who comes the
first time and immediately falls asleep? And to women who have difficulty
in tolerating all forms of artificial contraceptives, the Tao will have an added
attraction. For when a man has truly mastered the Tao of Loving, he
ejaculates only about once in several weeks and contraceptives become
almost meaningless. It is not too far-fetched to say that once the Tao of
Loving has become popular knowledge, all harmful artificial contraceptives
will become obsolete for many people. The Tao cannot do all the things its
seventh-century interpreters claimed for it, but it can give you the harmony
of Yin and Yang. This in turn produces peace of mind, a zest for life and a
slowing down of the ageing process.

4. *The importance of the right partner*
As we explained earlier, an unsympathetic and uncooperative woman can
make things difficult, even for an experienced man. For instance, a man
who has practised the Tao for many years will still have a problem if he has
an inhibited and dogmatic partner. This is one more reason why both
partners should know and practise the Tao of Loving. The woman should
at least understand terms like 'soft entry', 'ejaculation control', etc. Nearly
all ancient Taoist literature stressed the importance of finding the right
partner. In love-making, as in dancing or sport, no one can perform really
well with an uncooperative partner. This however does not mean you will
or have to attain complete harmony each time you make love, even with
an ideal partner. It is total effect that counts. Deep erotic kissing can help
to harmonize the Yin and Yang, but not all erotic kissing leads to intercourse. Some love sessions, however, should lead to complete harmony of

[2]   *Sexual Behaviour in the Human Male*, pp. 158–9.

111

Yin and Yang. In conventional terms, complete sexual harmony means orgasms and yet more orgasms for the woman — clitoral, vaginal, blended or multiple. The debate about the various type of female orgasm is irrelevant if you practise the Tao of Loving. When you can enjoy a thousand thrusts a day the argument becomes unimportant. The whole question of orgasm takes on a different aspect when a man can make love to a woman many times a day instead of only once a week.

Naturally, there are some people who will not have the appetite for this much love-making. That may be because they have never tried it. So long as the man abides by the advice on ejaculation control given in this book, he will experience not strain but pleasure. And his partner, once she has experienced the joy of loving as we have described it, will rarely be bored or tired of making love. Nor does this mean spending the whole day in bed. If each coition, including foreplay, takes about ten to twenty minutes, then even six coitions will take no more than two hours. Most couples spend more time watching television or going to a movie and they probably do not find it as satisfying. There are no rules for this kind of programme, you can spread your coitions out over twenty-four hours or enjoy them all at once, whichever you both enjoy most. The intensity of love-making will vary from time to time. Of course, you do not have to make love so many times every day.

5. *Male orgasm — the Tao of Loving way*

As we have mentioned, in Taoist theory an ejaculation is only a momentary sensation, like a thunderbolt or a burst of stored-up energy. If a man makes love regularly, then his sexual energies are harmonized and his need for ejaculation is greatly minimized. Loving, rather than being occasional and explosive, is continuous and flowing. Love-making should be like a good dinner. Each course should be exquisite in itself and, at the same time, should whet the appetite for the next dish until, at the end of the meal, you are fully satisfied. The satisfaction, though, is a result of the total experience and not just one of the parts. So it should be with love-making. According to both ancient Taoists and modern physicians, it is better to have small quantities of food on a regular basis than a huge meal once in a while. This concept should be thoroughly understood by both the man and woman if they wish to master the Tao quickly and completely.

6. *Some questions answered*

The only transformer and alchemist

113

That turns everything into gold is love.

The only magic against death,

Ageing, ordinary life, is love.[3]

Though Kinsey and Masters and Johnson's researches have made it easier for us to accept new ideas about love and sex, the Tao of Loving as a whole is still an astonishing concept to many Westerners. It astonished even a close friend when I began writing this book but now she is almost a Taoist.

Many questions will inevitably come in some readers' minds after reading something as different as this book. To anticipate some of these will undoubtedly help learning the Tao of Loving:

(1) What is the difference between Taoism as a philosophy and as a religion? There is a very great difference. Like many popular Eastern philosophies such as Buddhism and Confucianism, the concept of Taoism was gradually misinterpreted by some people to whom it became a form of religion and they built temples, adopted ceremonies and worshipped with images. The very thing that a true Taoist detests. In our book it is strictly Taoism as a philosophy that we are talking about.

(2) What is the Taoist concept of love? It has fewer romantic ingredients and more practical components than the existing Western concept. Generally a Taoist believes that physical harmony is indivisible from spiritual harmony. A couple who can make love ecstatically together are likely to provide each other with peace and harmony in every way and hence their loving attraction for each other may increase and become a more permanent one. Before they first made love, however, they may only have had slight loving attraction for each other, while the current Western concept is that a couple should romantically fall in love before they make love.

(3) Why does this book seem to have so little to say to the woman reader? All ancient Tao of Loving books were almost exclusively written to help men for the simple reason that men 'belong' to fire which is easily extinguished by women who 'belong' to water. We, however, believe that women can also benefit from knowing the Tao of Loving. But the fact remains that in the realm of love-making the man is still much more vulnerable and many are urgently in need of help. The main purpose of this book is therefore to offer assistance so that they may become better and healthier lovers. If we achieve this, many women will automatically benefit.

(4) Is the Tao of Loving medically sound and can this be proved? The seventh-century work of the great medical authority, Sun S'sû-Mo[4] — *Priceless Recipe* — has

---

[3] *The Diary of Anais Nin*, Vol. 4 (Harcourt Brace Jovanovich, New York, 1971), p.174.

[4] Sun lived from A.D. 581–682. His book was probably published during the middle of the seventh century. It has been a public property for more than thirteen centuries and yet no known dispute or even criticism existed against his theories on the Tao of Loving. Please do not think for a moment that the Chinese are hesitant to criticize even the most eminent authorities. To prove this point we can mention a small but interesting example of how a Ming (A.D. 1368–1644) pharmaceutical authority Li Shih-Chen has openly disputed Sun's view on walnut. In Li's famous book *Pen Ts'ao Kang Mu*, a monumental work on Chinese foods and drugs, Li mentioned that Sun made a mistake in saying that walnut was 'cold' in character and therefore too much eating might cause excessive sputum etc. Li said that time had proved Sun wrong in this respect.

never been challenged and, indeed, has been reprinted in China as recently as 1955, and Sun is held in high esteem in China today. Sun's theories are given in some detail in Chapter 4, Section 6 and in the 'Summing Up'. But we do not have to rely on a work first published over 1,200 years ago. The researches of Masters and Johnson over the last twenty years have confirmed much of the basic Tao of Loving theory and their work is being applied by many therapists and in many clinics throughout the world.

(5) What do you consider the most important attribute of this ancient way of loving? It is your famous second-century physician Galen who said: 'After coitus all animals are sad except women and cocks.' (In a Taoist physician's view this saying would be far more to the point if the word 'coitus' were changed to 'ejaculation'.) Nearly every man has experienced the devastating after-effect of ejaculation — the sudden feeling that he has lost nearly all interest in his woman, which may even lead him to wonder why he has ever loved her. Intuitively, most women quickly notice that their lover has become remote and indifferent. It is a well-known fact that many men fall soundly asleep almost instantly after ejaculation, leaving their partner feeling deserted and unsatisfied. In less permanent relationships the situation is even worse; the men often have the wish to leave immediately and many do. This is humiliating and deeply hurtful and if such ill feelings accumulate, they can easily turn into mutual hatred. The fact that we see surprisingly few happy faces everywhere tells us the prevalence of this dissatisfaction. People who are satisfied in love and sex are, as a rule, happy people. This at least partly explains why we have so much hatred and so little love left in our world today. The Tao of Loving with its methods of ejaculation control etc. could easily change all this. And this is what I consider the most important attribute of the Tao of Loving.

However, nearly all my female friends, being the more practical of the two sexes, have a different point of view. They consider the Tao of Loving provides them with unlimited freedom in caressing their men, and this is one of its two most important attributes. Before they knew the Tao they were, without exception, starved of loving affection which scarcely existed between them and their hard-pressed men. The Tao quickly changed that situation. The other equally important attribute which they unanimously agreed upon is the Tao of Loving as a way of birth control. One of them puts it succinctly: 'It is so wonderful to be able to make love whenever you want, even at midnight, without having to think of stupid chemicals and equipment, which make you sick, bother you and make you feel that love-making is no longer love-making!'

(6) Do these women miss men's ejaculation? Only a few feel strange in the very beginning, but they quickly become accustomed to it and begin to see all the overwhelming advantages.

(7) What makes so many men become indifferent and remote towards their women after ejaculation? The ancient Taoists believed that 'ching' (semen) is the driving force behind men's love for their women (indeed they even believed that 'ching' is man's most important life force). Once a man has ejaculated it is like letting air out of a tyre or balloon — he feels flat, especially so when he ejaculates with great frequency.

(8) Can you try to explain in modern terms the ancient belief that men 'belong' to fire and women 'belong' to water? It simply means that, in a conventional way of making love, men usually cannot easily satisfy their women and often exhaust themselves in

trying. This is common knowledge even in the Western world. In her popular book *Fear of Flying*, Erica Jong has made this amply clear. In a less direct way many others before her, such as Havelock Ellis, D.H. Lawrence, Aldous Huxley and Doris Lessing, have expressed the same view.

(9) How much does food affect love-making? Very much. So much so that one may even say that when men or women constantly eat unhealthy food they cannot possibly maintain a healthy and satisfying love life. We might add here that a beef-eater is not necessarily a better lover than a vegetarian. It all depends on their knowledge of what is and what is not wholesome to their own individual body.

(10) Can you give some simple and important reasons why the Tao is vital to both men and women's health and longevity? There are two obvious reasons why the Tao is beneficial to all. First, when both men and women can have as much loving as they need it is easy for them to maintain a happy and harmonious love life together. This harmony may even change their relationship with people all around them; kindness and sympathy will prevail, petty and poisonous thoughts of envy and jealousy will diminish. It is not difficult to see that this situation is beneficial to their well-being and hence to good health and longevity.

The second beneficial effect of maximum love-making is a healthy hormonal balance. Modern medicine has discovered that hormonal balance is vital to human well-being. In ancient Taoist terms this state is but one of the most important benefits of the harmony of Yin and Yang. The Taoists believed that the more one made love the easier a healthier level of hormonal balance could be maintained. Many physicians today are carrying out sex-steroid replacement therapy for patients who demand it. Such treatments striving for hormonal balance understandably entail a high price not only in terms of medical fees but also in terms of risking dangerous side-effects which often result from treatments of potent drugs such as artificial hormones. But why artificial steroids when, given a reasonable chance, our bodies are quite capable of making plenty of natural, incomparably cheaper and safer ones? Not only ample love-making can stimulate men, for example, to produce more testosterone to reach a high, healthier level. According to an interesting study carried out in 1974 at Max-Planck-Institute for Psychiatry in Munich by endocrinologist Karl M. Pirke M.D., psychiatrist Götz Kockott M.D. and psychologist Franz Dittman, that visual stimulation alone without ejaculation or coitus could appreciably increase men's testosterone level in the blood stream. A sexual movie of 30 minutes of petting, undressing, foreplay and coitus in various positions was the visual stimulation and its watching notably increased the testosterone level of 6 out of 8 men of between 21 and 34 years of age. It is reasonable to assume that this Munich study confirms the ancient Taoist belief that almost any form of stimulation between men and women such as kissing and caressing could be beneficial and ejaculation is not always necessary. When testosterone levels can be increased by visual stimulation alone, ample, actual love-making will of course be incomparably more effective in securing hormonal balance. Except, in the ancient Chinese view, a man cannot achieve this unless he has learned to regulate his ejaculation. Again this is common sense. As a result there will not be much love-making hence not much harmony of Yin and Yang. And this is the second obvious reason why the Tao is so important to men and women's health and longevity.

116

Summing Up: Some Personal Experiences

If you can make love a hundred times without emission you can live a long life.

SUN S'SÛ-MO

IN 1962 THE ACADEMY OF MEDICINE IN PEKING HELD A CEREMONIAL tribute to perhaps the greatest physician of ancient China, Sun S'sû-Mo, commemorating his contribution to the people. One of his many innovations, the inoculation for smallpox, alone must have saved millions of lives.

Sun S'sû-Mo not only helped others, he managed his own health extremely well too. He lived 101 years, from A.D. 581 to 682. And there is no doubt that he was the kind of man who practised what he preached. His advice, 'If you can make love one hundred times without emission you can live a long life,' must have partly contributed to his own longevity.

We specially mention Master Sun here again not only because his advice usually produced near magic results but also because he foresaw the most difficult obstacle a man must overcome before he can benefit from the Tao of Loving completely. He says in his *Priceless Recipe*:

> *When a man is in his youth*
> *He usually does not understand the Tao.*
> *Or even if he does hear or read about it,*
> *He is not likely to believe it fully and practise it.*
> *When he reaches his vulnerable old age,*
> *He will however realize the significance of the Tao.*
> *But by then it is often too late,*
> *For he is usually too sick to benefit fully from it.*

The sagacious Master Sun predicted almost exactly my fate 1,300 years later, except that I was lucky enough not to wait until it was too late to realize the significance of the Tao.

I was about sixteen when I first read about the Tao of Loving. But there was no opportunity to try it out (or rather I was too innocent to recognize

117

one or too timid to seize it) until I was eighteen. By that time, however, I had also read van de Velde's *Ideal Marriage* in translation. In many ways it was an excellent book, otherwise it would not have been so popular nearly all over the world. But unfortunately the author van de Velde made some grave mistakes, particularly when he advises men not to attempt coition unless they are prepared to ejaculate. And he attacked Marie Stopes savagely for her difference in opinion on the subject.

What young man of eighteen would rather not take van de Velde's advice of ejaculating each time than Master Sun's advice of one ejaculation out of one hundred coitions or even his much modified advice for a young man of twenty to ejaculate once every four days? Naturally I embraced van de Velde's advice like most impressionable young men would to escape from Master Sun's discipline of ancient 'tyranny'. Alas, I was to be punished heavily for twelve years for betraying the ancient wisdom!

As I have said, I was in my athletic eighteen years and I was in love for the first time. I tried my utmost to please my girl, according to van de Velde's advice. Though we were officially unmarried (during those war years in China relationships were about as free as today's in Western Europe), we lived together like man and wife with our parents' blessing. I was shortly to go to the war and we spent more than two summer months in a resort-like old city called Tsunyi (it is a well-known historical town now, for Chairman Mao made it for a period his headquarters during the Long March years). It is an ancient walled city located on a plateau. During summer it has exceptionally charming weather. It was almost constantly about 70°F. and the sun shone nearly every day. Usually it rained a little every night before dawn so that the air was always pure and refreshing. Because of this ideal weather foodstuff of all kinds was plentiful. It was in these beautiful surroundings that we had our long 'honeymoon'.

What was the result? The word 'helpless' perhaps could sum up the pathetic situation. Why 'helpless' when both of us were healthy, very much in love and in an ideal situation far removed from all visible earthly miseries — besides, we had van de Velde's book for guidance? Well, the real problem was van de Velde's obsessive advice concerning ejaculation such as: '... reaches culmination in the ejaculation of semen into the vagina and in the approximately simultaneous orgasm or summit of enjoyment in both partners'.

So I tried very hard to follow van de Velde's advice. Every time we made love I ejaculated and we made love usually about three times a day. But no

119

matter how hard I tried it seemed that I was only able to arouse her appetite for more loving. Three ejaculations daily nearly every day for more than two months was about the utmost any young man could do. In any case I could do no more no matter how nourishing the food I was eating. I was constantly exhausted and I slept long hours. But I could still see that she was not really satisfied.

Though I had some misgiving towards van de Velde's guidance at that point, I did not give up his advice for another twelve years. All my experiences during those years were more or less the same. Dissatisfied love partners — no matter how hard I tried and how exhausted I became. My general health was very different from that of my athletic youth, and it was not one minute too soon that I rejected for ever van de Velde's advice and returned to the ancient wisdom.

Now I am nearly sixty, the age many men have stopped making love entirely. Yet unless I am travelling alone I usually make love several times a day. Often on a Sunday I make love two or three times in the morning and then go cycling for nearly the whole day, about twenty or thirty miles, and then make love again before going to sleep. The result is that I am not in the least exhausted, and my health could not be better or my mind more tranquil. And above all the helpless situation of lying beside an unsatisfied mate no longer exists. What is the reason for this change?

The answer is that I now practise what the Taoist physician Sun S'sû-Mo prescribed 1,300 years ago: 'Love one hundred times without emission.'

Postscript

by Joseph Needham

Address for Caius Chapel (Whit Sunday, 1976)

In Cambridge one day my friend Joseph Needham showed me an address, his last as Master, which he gave in the Chapel of Caius College, Cambridge, on Whit Sunday 1976. We felt that there were so many echoes in it of what has been said in this book that it would be good to reprint it as a postscript here. Many of my readers will necessarily be people who have grown up in traditional Christendom, and for them this address has a special message, in tune with what I have said in this book.   J.C.

WE ALL KNOW THAT PASSAGE IN THE THIRTEENTH CHAPTER OF THE FIRST Epistle of Paul to the Corinthians: 'If I speak with the tongues of men and of angels, but have not love, I am become as a sounding brass or a clanging cymbal. And if I have the gift of prophecy, and understand all mysteries and knowledge, and if I have all faith so as to move mountains, but have not love, I am nothing. And if I give all my goods to feed the poor, and my body to be burned, but have not love, it profiteth me nothing.'

What really *is* this experience of love? How can one talk about it without clichés, without bathos, without archness, without vulgarity? I don't exactly know, but I shall have a try, because, so far as I can see, it is the one fundamental thing which our religion is all about, and perhaps what all the developed religions are all about. Surely it was the revelation that came to the disciples on that first Whit Sunday. At every liturgy we hear the two Great Commandments by which Jesus superseded the old Jewish Law, indeed perhaps all laws of every kind: 'Thou shalt love the Lord thy God with all thy heart and with all thy mind and with all thy strength, and thou shalt love thy neighbour as thyself.'[1] They were not new with him for they go back to the seventh century B.C. at least,[2] but it was he who gave them universal authority as the essence of his teaching. I should like to deal with

[1] Matthew 22, 37ff; Mark 12, 29ff.
[2] Deuteronomy 6, 5 and Leviticus 19, 18 respectively.

121

the second one first, because it's the one nearest home, and we shall see whether the first will grow out of it.

I have long been profoundly convinced that one of the greatest mistakes of Christian thinking through the centuries has been that sharp separation so many theologians and spiritual guides have made between 'love carnall' and 'love seraphick'. There are really no sharp lines of distinction between 'sacred' and 'profane' love, between *eros*, *phileia*, and *agape*. I believe that this division was essentially a Manichaean belief intruding into the Christian gospel, the product of those Gnostics who believed that the material world of things and bodies was utterly and irredeemably evil; and that the God of disembodied life and light whom they worshipped was not a creator, or the Creator, at all. The Creator had been an evil demiurge, and everything in the world made by him was evil and to be renounced. That is certainly not our religion. Yet we do urgently need today a new theology of sexuality, partly because the Church was so permeated by these Manichaean ideas through the centuries, but partly also because of the fundamental new knowledge which man has gained since the seventeenth century about the nature of generation, and the structure and functions of his own mind. We even need a new system of moral theology, a guide to saint-hood, conceived in the light of all the knowledge we now have, and not built upon tradition and ignorance. As Samuel Keen has written: 'Though unfortunately most of organised Christianity remains Gnostic in its attitudes towards the body and the natural world, the truly Christian God is for passionateness, fire, new life, life more abundant, the resurrection of the body.' And in the words of Norman Pittenger: 'Man is created to be, intended by God to be, a lover, however much by his pride and self-will he has frustrated that intention . . . The clue is love.' Or again: 'Man's destiny, under God, is to become in full realization the lover he was meant to be.'

Perhaps the most startlingly epigrammatic way of putting my theme is in that saying that 'the only immorality is lack of love.' I would like this evening to accompany you in a kind of meditation on the nature of love as we know it in its most intense forms, which it generally takes, though not always, between people of different sexes. Let us remind ourselves of what it can be like. Rabbi Yitzchak of Akko, blessed be his memory, gives us another challenge when he says: 'He who has never loved a woman is likened to an ass or worse, for all service to God must begin with the discrimination and further sublimation of lofty emotions.'

Yes, the lover is in ecstasy, which in Greek means that he or she is standing outside himself or herself, 'being beside oneself' as people say. Such is love at high temperature; the enthusiasm of lovers on the heights of passion. Again, enthusiasm means that they have a *theos*, a god inside, 'possessed by some god', as the Greeks used to say.

Let us remember some of the phenomena. Bliss can come anywhere, at any time. It can illuminate the workaday instruments of the laboratory bench. It can happen when the person one loves meets one's train or plane after a long journey. It can give the feeling that paradise has come down to earth when two people are, for example, cooling a melon in the pool of a mountain stream. And who would suppose that the sudden idea of turning in together for a cup of morning coffee would set alight the torches and sound all the trumpets of the utmost happiness that man can know. Fortunate are those lovers if they have the ability to play together, almost like children, forgetting the roles of Parent or Adult, as modern psychology knows so well. Possibly this is one of the many meanings of the saying that in order to enter the kingdom of heaven people should become as little children. Then again there is the theme of pursuit. I knew someone who had a vivid recurring fantasy or waking dream of pursuing one that he loved all over the islands of the Hongkong archipelago and their roads, almost catching up but never quite. And as in all these other things I describe, the theme of the love of God is never far away, sometimes it's almost indistinguishable; in this case the idea in Francis Thompson's poem 'The Hound of Heaven'. I often like to quote that wonderful verse written by the sufi Abu-'l-Fazl al-Allāmī at the court of Akbar in Delhi in the late sixteenth century:

> *Sometimes I frequent the Christian cloister and sometimes the mosque*
> *But it is Thou whom I search for from temple to temple.*
> *Thine elect have no dealings with heresy or orthodoxy*
> *For neither of these stands beside the screen of Thy truth.*
> *Speculation to the heretic, theology to the orthodox,*
> *But the dust of the rose-petal belongs to the heart of the perfume-seller.*

Such is the mystic's search, hindered by no gates, no barriers.

But anyone who thinks that the bliss of human union may be unalloyed is in for a disillusion. Suffering seems inseparable from serious loving, and sometimes it blends into absolute agony. There is, for example, obviously, the pain of separation, when thousands of miles of space intervene between the lover and his beloved. I remember being much touched long ago by a passage in the *Lü Shih Chhun Chhiu*, written about 240 B.C., in which the author is trying to demonstrate the reality of action at a distance, and gives as an example that if a girl was living in the east in Chhi State, while her lover was far away in the west in Chhin, if anything happened to him she would be sure to be aware of it.

Then there is the mystery of evanescence, the agony of transitoriness. Nothing remains quite the same. People age and change, physical passion endures only for a limited time. How awful is transitoriness! Lovers visiting Buddhist temples, or even Buddhist galleries in museums, can know the full pain of this, that nothing lasts; 'tout passe, tout casse, tout lasse.' Of course it was this evanescence on which the Lord Buddha, as we call him in Ceylon, founded his whole philosophy; a solution which depended upon the annihilation of desire. Christianity, as I see it, says rather that people should have desire for love and life, and have it more abundantly, especially give it more abundantly.

Of course when passionate love is mutual, and can for a time be satisfied and fulfilled, the very gates of paradise seem to be opened, and joy comes down like the City of God to earth. But alas, there are so many circumstances in which love relationships are doomed; for example, one so easily gets the Romeo–Juliet situation, as in *West Side Story*, when all the onlookers are moved to curse, crying out: 'A plague on both your houses.' Or it may be that the patterns of life, of work, the careers and circumstances, the things that matter most to the two individuals, won't fit in, as in that famous film *Brief Encounter*. It is then that dreadful destinies may be in wait for those who refuse to accept the patterns which life has formed for them, those who 'rebel against God's will' as some of our forefathers might have put it. There is a wonderful piece about this in Auden's 'New Year Letter':

> *Oh but it happens every day.*
> *To someone. Suddenly the way*
> *Leads straight into their native lands,*
> *The* temenos' *small wicket stands*
> *Wide open, shining at the centre,*
> *The well of life, and they may enter . . .*
> *Direct to that magnetic spot,*
> *Nor will, nor willing-not-to will,*
> *For there is neither good nor ill*
> *But free rejoicing energy;*
> *Yet any time, how casually,*
> *Out of his organised distress*

An accidental happiness,
Catching man off his guard, will blow him
Out of his life in time to show him
The field of Being where he may
Unconscious of Becoming, play
with the Eternal Innocence
In unimpeded utterance.
But perfect Being has ordained
It must be lost to be regained
And in its orchards grows the tree
And fruit of human destiny,
And man must eat it and depart
At once with gay and grateful heart,
Obedient, reborn, re-aware;
For if he stop an instant there,
The sky grows crimson with a curse,
The flowers change colour for the worse,
He hears behind his back the wicket
Padlock itself, from the dark thicket,
The chuckle with no healthy cause . . .
. . . And helpless, sees the crooked claws
Emerging into view and groping
For handholds on the low round coping,
As horror clambers from the well,
For he has sprung the trap of hell.

Here then is another sort of agony, the fact that life which has brought the lovers together is ineradicably separating them as each one has to go his, and her, own way.   A wealth of traditional Chinese poetry hangs upon this, the ineluctable parting of friends. Perhaps Goethe put it most shortly in his 'Iphigenia' when he wrote:

'Und keine Zeit und keine Macht zerstückelt

Geprägte Form, die lebend sich entwickelt.'

(And neither Time nor any Power can break in pieces

Those long-grown patterns that life itself has wrought.)

Yet this is where the community of love comes in, and those famous phrases: 'We are all members one of another,' and that we should 'bear one another's burdens'.[3]   Lovers bereft will find that they are not alone in the

[3]   Ephesians 4, 25 and Galatians 6, 2 respectively.

world, and that deep consolations can come from other friends, who will treat them with loving care as if wounded in some inevitable accident. This is the kind of thing so poignantly expressed by Rupert Brooke in his verses:

And I shall find some girl, perhaps,
And a better one than you,
With eyes as wise, but kindlier,
And lips as soft but true —
And I daresay she will do.

But help will come also from the revolutionary army of all those who fight compassionately for better things for their brothers and sisters, that invisible Church of the believers in practical loving and caring. There is a memorable passage on this in Day Lewis's 'Noah and the Waters'.

. . . He says goodbye
Too much, but not to love. For loving now shall be
The close handclasp of the waters about his trusting keel,
Buoyant they make his home, and lift his heart high;
Among their marching multitude he never shall feel lonely.
Love is for him no longer a soft and garden sigh
Ruffling at evening the petalled composure of the senses,
But a wind all hours and everywhere he nowise can deny.

The fact is that no human being can ever have enough love, handclasps and physical contact too, or better still ever give enough. At the end of Graham Greene's *The Honorary Consul* Charlie says: 'There's never anything wrong in love, Clara, it just happens. In the end it may not matter very much exactly who it was with.'

So far we have been looking at everything from a rather subjective point of view; let us now turn for a moment to a more objective one. Modern scientific psychology and physiology have taught us a number of things which Augustine of Hippo and Thomas Aquinas didn't quite know. We realize now that in the human organism there is a kind of power-house of emotions, the id, pouring forth psychological energy of two kinds, libido and mortido. The former leads to love, affection, sexual drive and co-operativeness; the latter generates hatred, aggression and divisiveness. All loving friendship hangs upon this — 'Behold how sweet and pleasant a thing it is, for brethren to dwell together in unity.'[4] One would be tempted to call these two forms of energy positive and negative, like Yang and Yin, if it were not for the fact that in traditional Chinese philosophy perfection

[4] Psalms 133.

126

resided in their optimum balance — and actually that might not be so untrue in this present case. Then libido and mortido can both act outwards or inwards. If the libido is directed inwards, one gets narcissism and hypochondriac states; if the mortido is directed inwards one gets asceticism and masochism, contrasting with the sadism of the outward direction. The ego is the organizing element in the human spirit, trying as it were to operate the controls, and sometimes failing; while the ideals which it has 'in mind' as one might say (and which may be quite wrong ideals) are summed up by the term super-ego. The function of our religion therefore, and perhaps of all the higher religions, is to encourage outwardly-directed libido and inwardly-directed mortido, though always subject to rational control, as against unreasonable affections and undue mortifications. It is quite easy to see how these two drives should have arisen in evolution. For the former, libido, was obviously connected with the propagation of the species, while the latter, mortido, was directed to the preservation of the life of the individual. If Jesus was truly man, he had all this machinery too.

When we think in terms like these we can understand the manifestations of the emotional life much better. Uncontrolled by the ego and the super-ego, libido goes forth to other human beings, glorious and terrible 'like an army with banners',[5] but the individual has to learn something which is much harder than requited love, namely the practice of love without hope or expectation of return. This may be necessary in many human situations, and surely this must have been what Jesus's love of men and women was like. Or it may be a ladder towards the love of God. Rabbi Yitzchak, of blessed memory, whom I quoted just now, has a story in his *Reshith Hokhmah* about a poor man who fell in love with a princess when he saw her bathing in the river. When he declared his love to her, its immensity filled her with compassion, but she answered that it would only be in the graveyard that she would be able to meet him and be his own. She meant by this that it was the only place where rich and poor, aristocrat and beggar, would be equals. But he understood it to be an assignation, and he went and waited for her there. Day by day he meditated on the form of his beloved with increasing fervour, and this led him on to contemplate the divine in all its forms, that which gives them such beauty and grace, and so (as we should say in China) he gradually obtained the Tao. Now this was a story in what was the Platonic tradition, but there are also others, such as the Tantric, in which men and women may rise to mystical union with

5   Canticles 6, 4.

the universe, and with God, through their love for other human beings. In Tantric Buddhism the *shakti*, or feminine counterpart, is the source of all the wisdom and energy of the divinity. It is fascinating to find Wisdom, Hagia Sophia, depicted in our own scriptures as a woman, a *shakti*, almost a goddess, not a man.

> *Send Wisdom forth out of thy holy heaven*
> *And from the throne of thy glory let her come . . .*
> *For she knoweth all things and hath understanding thereof . . .*
> *And she shall guard me in her glory . . .*[6]

I spoke earlier on about the agony of separation, but there is also the agony of rejection – can you go on loving when someone you intensely love rejects you? That someone perhaps prefers someone else, perhaps partly or for a while. Can you go on loving when he or she is sunk in neurotic depression, or some other situation, when either for social or neuro-chemical reasons he or she can no longer feel love to love you back? All love which falls short of these heights is imperfect love, which is why there is such evil in possessiveness and jealousy. Some lovers stifle those they love, grudging them even variation of companionship. But people are not things. As the Confucian *Analects* say: 'the scholar is not an instrument.' If we would only realize it, possessiveness and jealousy are almost always counter-productive. In a most Taoist way they repel instead of attracting, for freedom alone is the atmosphere in which true love can flourish. I have long suspected that we should replace in our thinking both 'love carnall' and 'love seraphick' by 'love heroick'.

Surely it was this height of love, this 'love heroick', which we find in the life of our own supreme spiritual guide, the Jesus Chrismatos, the Anointed One, of the Gospels. People are always singing hymns about love (like 'Love divine, all loves excelling') but they don't give enough time to analysing exactly what it means. I think what I am really trying to say this evening is that all this has to be translated into terms of Jesus's love for all sorts of people, men and women, young and old. As I walk around the Cambridge streets I am often deeply oppressed by the fact that sometimes I find humanity as a whole so unattractive. Probably the mistake arises because there's no such thing as 'humanity as a whole', just as nothing is ever 'merely' anything. Each single person that I pass should be visualized as a human being, a brother or a sister, my friend or my lover, capable of wonderful selflessness, amazing insights, and admirable actions. How truly

[6] Wisdom 8 and 9.

divine it would be — how truly divine it was — that this extreme intensity of love which I have been trying to describe, should be directed to all men and women without exception. In the words of the old Cornish Carol:

Tomorrow shall be my dancing day
I would my true love did so chance
To see the moral of my play
And come into the general dance . . .

They were all his true loves. If we are going to glimpse this at all we can only visualize it in terms of the experiences which we have had in our own lives, and I should like to suggest this awareness to you, even though some of us here have many years yet before them, containing (I hope and pray) much happiness, much ecstasy and much to go through.

Finally, there is love towards God Himself. We are dreadfully used to that phrase 'God so loved us that he gave his only-begotten Son etc.,[7] but I don't think that we need to envisage things only in terms of the incarnation. That idea indeed Christians will never renounce; it is their perpetual cause for rejoicing — but we can take a still broader view. Look at the whole course of evolution which has led up to humanity. Some no doubt prefer to think in terms of chance and necessity acting in a perfectly meaningless universe, but for me this is impossible. For me it is God that has raised us up from the dust of stars and suns in this incredible universe, through untold hundreds or thousands of centuries since the beginning of our solar system. And very likely we are not the only ones either, because it seems now not merely possible, or probable, but almost certain, that there must be untold millions more beings very like us on other planets in other solar systems in other galaxies, of which as yet we know almost nothing at all. Long ago in Victorian times Francis Thompson had another remarkable poem on this subject, and later on C.S. Lewis wrote an outstanding science fiction novel, *Perelandra*, on a similar theme, though he was a good deal more traditional in his theology than I am. I said at the beginning that theology today has to come to terms with modern physiology and psychology, and here the same thing applies — it has to come to terms with astronomy and cosmology. To say in the liturgy *hagios, ischyros, athanatos* (holy, mighty, holy and immortal) was always right, but when one thinks of what we know now about novae and supernovae, galaxies millions of light-years apart, red dwarfs, and black holes, how right it was, far, far more justified than anyone of old can have imagined in their wildest dreams.

---

[7] John 3, 16.

So finally what about 'cosmic libido'? I said just now that libido leads to co-operativeness, so that if the principle of increasing organization has been the key-note of evolution on our earth and in our solar system, then libido must have been winning the day over mortido for aeons past — Ahura-Mazda triumphing perpetually over Ahriman. This brings us back again to another favourite theme of ancient writers, most epigrammatically expressed in Dante perhaps when he spoke of 'l'amor que muove il sole e l'altre stelle' (That love which moves the Sun and the other Stars). Surely we can see God's love to us in the ever-continued triumph of the principle of aggregation and organization; the relative successes of the cohesive binding forces in nature, rather than the disintegrating and destructive ones. Just look at any form of life — a nemertine worm, a ctenophore, a sea-urchin pluteus, the miracle is that *it holds together*! I remember many years ago being astonished that the great Lucretius prefaced his immortal poem *De Rerum Natura* with an invocation to Aphrodite as the goddess of union, cohesion, solidarity, aggregation, reproduction and mutual love — libido in fact, though he did not use that word. She was the mainspring, he said, of the universe — *quae quoniam rerum natura sola gubernas.* These are the triumphs, then, that I wanted to celebrate tonight; the overwhelming love of Jesus for all mankind, and the love of God to us, who moulded us out of the furnaces of suns and stars to love and serve Him, by loving each other.

Let me end then with the Collect for Quinquagesima from our own Book of Common Prayer

> O Lord, who has taught us that all our doings without love are nothing worth, send Thy holy spirit and pour into our hearts that most excellent gift of love, the very bond of peace and all virtues, without which whomsoever liveth is .counted dead before Thee; grant this for Thine only Son Jesus Christ's sake. Amen

June 5th, 1976

130

Bibliography I : *Chinese Texts*

Su Nü Ching
Su Nü Fang
Yü Fang Pi Chü
Tung Hsüan Tzu by Li Tung Hsien (Sui or T'ang)
T'ien Ti Yin Yang Chiao Huen Ta Lo Fu by Pai Hseng-Cheng (T'ang)
    The above five books are the 1914 editions edited by Yeh Te Hui, an eminent scholar from Hunen. The authors of the first three are not known, but their date is certainly pre-T'ang, probably Han.
Priceless Recipe by Sun S'sû-Mo (T'ang) – 1955 reprint of Northern Sung Dynasty edition.
Chi Chi Chen Ching by Lu Tung Pin (T'ang)
Hsiu Chen Yen I by Wu Hsien (Han)
Su Nu Miao Lun Anonymous
    The above four books were reprinted by van Gulik. Only fifty copies of these works are available, distributed among the major libraries of the world.
Pen Ts'ao Kang Mu by Li Shih Chen (Ming)
I Hsin Fang, compiled and edited by Tamba Yasuyori, a famous Japanese physician of Chinese descent in A.D. 984. The work consists of extracts from several hundred Chinese Books of the T'ang period and earlier. Here I have used the 1955 Chinese edition.
Han Wei Ts'ung Shu: 96 works by various authors such as the famous poet T'ao Ch'ien and the Taoist Ko Hung of the Chin period (A.D. 265–420).
Shih Chi (Historical Record) by Ssuma Ch'ien (Han)
Ch'ien Han Shu by Pau Ku (Han)
Hou Han Shu by Fan Yeh (Lui Sung period, A.D. 450)
Tao Tê Ching by Li Erh (Chou)
Jou Pu Tuan by Li Yu (Ming)
Hsi Hsiang Chi by Wang Shih-Fu (Yuan)
Chuang-Tzu by Chung Chou (Chou)

Bibliography II: *English Texts*

Appleton, J.L.T., *Bacterial Infection* (Philadelphia, 1950), 4th edition.

Bell, Davidson and Scarborough, *Textbook of Physiology and Biochemistry* (E. & S. Livingstone, Edinburgh and London, 1965), 6th edition.

Beurdeley, Michel, *The Clouds and the Rain; The Art of Love in China* (H. Hammond, London, 1969). Published in the U.S. as *Chinese Erotic Art* (C.E. Tuttle, Rutland, Vermont, 1969).

Brodie, Fawn M., *The Devil Drive: A Life of Sir Richard Burton* (W.W. Norton Co., New York, 1967).

Caprio, Frank S., *Variations in Sexual Behaviour* (Citadel Press, New Jersey, 1967; Calder Books, London, 1970).

Carpenter, Edward, *Love's Coming-of-Age* (Allen & Unwin, London, 1906; Folcroft, New York, 1912).

Cattier, Michel, *The Life and Work of Wilhelm Reich*, translated by Ghislain Boulanger (Horizon Press, New York, 1972; Avon Books, New York, 1973).

Chartham, Robert, *Advice to Men* (Tandem Books, London, 1971; New American Library, New York, 1971).

Chen Ken-Ch'ing and Robert W. Smith, *T'ai Chi* (Tuttle, Tokyo, 1967).

Chessner, Eustace, *The Human Aspects of Sexual Deviation* (Jarrolds Publishers, London, 1971).

Danielsson, Bengt, *Love in the South Sea* (Reynal, New York, 1956).

Darling, Lois and Louis, *The Science of Life* (World Publishing Co., Cleveland and New York, 1961).

de Beauvoir, Simone, *Old Age* (Weidenfeld & Nicolson, London, 1972). Published in the U.S. as *Coming of Age* (Putnam, New York, 1972).
The Second Sex (Knopf, New York, 1967; Jonathan Cape, London, 1968).

de Chardin, Pierre Teilhard, *Towards the Future*, translated by René Hague (Collins, London, 1975).

Diczfalusy, Egon and Borrell, Ulf (eds), *Control of Human Fertility*, 15th Nobel symposium (Almqvist & Wiksell, Stockholm, 1971).

Dunn, Nell, *Talking to Women* (Macgibbon & Kee, London, 1963; International Publications Service, New York, 1965).

Ellenberger, Henri, *The Discovery of the Unconscious* (Basic Books, New York, 1970).

Ellis, Havelock, *Studies in the Psychology of Sex* (Random House, New York).

Fisher, Seymour, *The Female Orgasm* (Basic Books, New York, 1972; Allen Lane, London, 1973).

Fromm, Erich, *The Art of Loving* (Harper & Row, New York, 1956; Allen & Unwin, London, 1957).

Greer, Germaine, *The Female Eunuch* (MacGibbon & Kee, London, 1970; McGraw-Hill, New York, 1971).

Gulik, R.H. van, *Sexual Life in Ancient China* (E.J. Brill, Leiden, 1961; Humanities Press, Atlantic Highlands, N.J., rev. ed., 1974).

Hodin, J.P., *Edward Munch* (Thames & Hudson, London, 1972; Praeger Publishers, New York, 1972).

Huxley, Aldous, *The Art of Seeing* (Penguin Books, Harmondsworth, 1963; Montana Books, Seattle, 1974).

Island (Harper & Row, New York, 1962; Penguin Books, Harmondsworth, 1970).

Jong, Erica, *Fear of Flying* (Holt, Rinehart & Winston, New York, 1973; Panther Books, London, 1976).

Josephson, Eric and Mary (eds), *Man Alone* (Dell Publishing Co., New York, 1968).

Kama Sutra Vatsyayana, translated by Sir Richard Burton (Allen & Unwin, London, 1963; E.P. Dutton, New York, 1964).

Kaplan, Helen Singer, *The New Sex Therapy* (Baillière Tindall, London, 1974).

Kinsey, Pomeroy and Martin, *Sexual Behaviour in the Human Male* (W.B. Saunders, London and Philadelphia, 1948).

Sexual Behaviour in the Human Female (W.B. Saunders, London and Philadelphia, 1953).

Kronhausen, Phyllis and Eberhard, *Erotic Art* (Grove Press, New York, 1961; W.H. Allen, London, 1971).

Labhart, Alexis, *Clinical Endocrinology* (Springer-Verlag, New York; Heidelberg, Berlin, 1974).

Lin Yutang, *The Wisdom of China* (Michael Joseph, London, 1963; Modern Library, New York, 1963).

Lindsey, Judge Ben B., *The Companionate Marriage* (Boni & Liveright, New York, 1927).

Linneé, Birgitt, *Sex and Society in Sweden* (Jonathan Cape, London, 1968; Harper & Row, New York, 1972).

Mailer, Norman, *The Prisoner of Sex* (Little, Brown & Co., Boston, 1971).

Marples, Mary, 'Life of Human Skin', *Scientific American*, January 1969.

Masters, R.E.L. and Benjamin, Harry, M.D., *The Prostitute in Society* (Mayflower-Dell, London, 1966).

Masters and Johnson, *Human Sexual Inadequacy* (Churchill, London, 1970; Little, Brown & Co., Boston, 1970).

Human Sexual Response (Churchill, London, 1966; Little, Brown & Co., Boston, 1966).

Menninger, Karl, *Man Against Himself* (Harcourt Brace Jovanovich, New York, 1972).

Millett, Kate, *Sexual Politics* (Hart-Davis, London, 1971; Avon Books, New York, 1971).

Morehouse, Lawrence E. and Gross, Leonard, *Total Fitness* (Simon & Schuster, New York, 1975).

Myrdal, Jan, *Confessions of a Disloyal European* (Vintage Books, New York, 1969).

Needham, Joseph, *Science and Civilization in China* (7 vols) (Cambridge University Press, Cambridge, 1954–).

Nefzawi, Shaykh, *The Perfumed Garden*, translated by Sir Richard Burton (Luxor Press, London, 1963).

Peel, John and Potts, Malcolm, *Contraceptive Practice* (Cambridge University Press, Cambridge, 1969).

Rawson, Philip, *Erotic Art of the East* (Weidenfeld & Nicolson, London, 1973).

Reich, Wilhelm, *The Function of the Orgasm* (Panther Books, London, 1972; Farrar, Straus & Giroux, New York, 1973).

Reik, Theodor, *Of Love and Lust* (Farrar, Straus & Cudahy, New York, 1957).

Robinson, Paul A., *The Freudian Left* (Harper & Row, New York, 1969).

Russell, Bertrand, *Autobiography* (Allen & Unwin, London, 1929; Little, Brown & Co., Boston, 1967).

Marriage and Morals (Allen & Unwin, London, 1929; Liveright, New York, new ed., 1970).

Rycroft, C., *Reich* (Fontana Modern Masters, London, 1971; Viking Press, New York, 1972).

Sand, Richard, *Things Your Mother Never Told You* (Avon Books, New York, 1972).

Schafer, Edward, *The Divine Woman* (University of California Press, Los Angeles, 1973).

Singer, Irving, *The Goals of Human Sexuality* (Wildwood House, London, 1973; W.W. Norton, New York, 1973).

Smith, Bradly and Weng Wan-Go, *China, A History in Art* (Studio Vista, London, 1973).

Stopes, Marie, *Married Love* (Hogarth Press, London, 1952).

Wise Parenthood, (Hogarth Press, London, 1952).

Pálos, Stephan, *The Chinese Art of Healing* (McGraw Hill, New York, 1971; Bantam Books, New York, 1972).

Velde, H. van de, *Ideal Marriage* (Heinemann Medical, London, 1965; Ballantine, New York, 1975).

Watts, Alan W., *Nature, Man and Woman* (Wildwood House, London, 1973).

Wilson, Colin, *The God of the Labyrinth* (Mayflower, London, 1971).

Origin of the Sexual Impulse (Arthur Barker, London, 1963).

Index